ARDUINO PROGRAMMING

A Comprehensive Beginners Guide to Learn Arduino Programming from A - Z

Preface

This book is written purposefully for those designers who are so are passionate about Arduino programming as well as circuit building. The topics covered therein deeply depicts what it takes to be an expert in electronics building. This book best suit those who are still "green" in Arduino designs as this is a complete describe from A-Z of Arduino learning. Right from installing Arduino IDE platform on your Personal Computer, building circuits on Arduino plus a breadboard. The codes (sketches) to control these designs are also laid out in this book. There are numerous examples, easy to follow and composed of most available electronic components.

Okay now let us face it, design, simulate and build prototypes for future electronics.

Table of Contents

Chapter 1

INTRODUCTION

Chapter Objectives

By the end of this chapter, the learner is expected to:

1. Define Arduino with regards to programming world in the light of electronics.

2. Describe fully the various types of Arduino boards available in the market, explain market costs, applications and differences and similarities.

3. Highlight intensively the evolution of Arduino coding, various stages of development, origin and future expectations.

Definition of Arduino

Arduino simply implies an open-source (easily accessible and manipulatable software) commonly referred to as a prototype that allows integration of computer programs with a circuit board. The programs or rather codes are written in a programming language (C++, Java, C, Python) then loaded through a ready-made platform called Arduino IDE (Integrated Development Environment) that transforms the codes into a language common to a hardware. The IDE communicates with the breadboard through issue of commands which when executed, the result is evident on the board.

An Arduino board

Arduino Key Features

❖ Most of the Arduino boards available in market are able to take in both digital and analog input signals either from the IDE or an external source e.g. Vibrating spring, sound of cymbal, rotation of a wheel. The signal is then transformed into the desired output that could be an LED being turned ON/OFF, starting a motor, connecting to a server, controlling motion of an object or obtaining data from another source.

❖ Most Arduino boards can be controlled remotely from a computer harboring an Arduino IDE (Integrated Development Environment). The user only need to upload instructions and thereby controlling Arduino board functions.

❖ Most of the existing or previous programmable circuit boards require an external hardware commonly referred to as a programmer. Arduino on the contrary does not requires any other hardware and therefore the user can easily input instructions through a USB cable.

❖ Arduino IDE has been simplified and is user-friendly since one only requires basic knowledge on C++ programming language. Additionally, the software has a self-debugging mechanism for troubleshooting and correcting errors on codes.

❖ Surely, the invention of Arduino is a great achievement as it breaks the more complex work of having to deal with micro-controllers. The whole system has been integrated into a small package which is portable, easy to handle, program, compatible with most of the existing hardware and easily accessible all the globe.

Arduino Evolution

Arduino was introduced into the market by a group of Engineers under the umbrella of Banzi Massimo, an Italian citizen in the year 2005. This was as a result of his desire to create a platform to enable engineers create and simulate hardware projects more easily and with least cost. Since then other companies have been coming up with Arduino clones compatible with the original one but with minor variations. If you are searching for an original Arduino package, make sure it bears the name Arduino with the two-eyed symbol labelled + and -. Maybe one can inquire form the original company itself in Italy. It is with high regard to highlight the fact that Arduino currently is available in various board shapes as discussed in the next section.

Types of Arduino Boards

Arduino can be confusing at times when one wants to prototype projects and inventions due to the vast types of boards currently available in the market. Armatures in the field of electronics and programming may assume that there is only one Arduino board. This is not the case as there are numerous types from the official Arduino board plus thousands of clones from competing companies. Most students at times opt to acquire clone Arduino boards since they are cheaply produced translating to a low market price. For me, original material still outstands whatever the price, cheap is expensive.

Currently, there are different types of Arduino boards based on the kind of microcontroller used. However, all these types of Arduino boards use Arduino IDE when they are being programmed. The differences are also manifest with regards to: Number of inputs and outputs, speed, form factor and voltage level. The number input and output terminals determines the number of sensors, number of LEDs and buttons that can be used on a specific Arduino board. The voltage levels here can be 3.8 volts or 5 volts and above.

The various classifications are discussed below:

1. Arduino Boards based on ATMEGA328 microcontroller technology

a. LilyPad Arduino: this is simply a board least modification. Key characteristics include:

- Operating voltage level: 3.3 volts

- Speed of the Clock: 8 MHz

- Number of Digital input/output terminals: 9

- Analog input terminals: 4

- Pulse-Width Modulation power: 5

- Programming Interface: FTDI (compatible header)

b. LilyPad Arduino 328: This consists of a main board with key characteristics:

- Operating voltage level: 3.3 volts

- Speed of the Clock: 8 MHz

- Number of Digital input/output terminals: 15

- Analog input terminals: 6

- Pulse-Width Modulation power: 6

- Programming Interface: FTDI (compatible header)

c. Arduino Fio: Key features are highlighted below:

- Operating voltage level: 3.3 volts

- Speed of the Clock: 8 MHz

- Number of Digital input/output terminals: 14

- Analog input terminals: 4

- Pulse-Width Modulation power: 6

- Programming Interface: FTDI (compatible header)

d. Arduino Ethernet: Key features:

- Operating voltage level: 5.0 volts

- Speed of the Clock: 16 MHz

- Number of Digital input/output terminals: 14

- Analog input terminals: 6

- Pulse-Width Modulation power: 6

- Programming Interface: FTDI (compatible header)

e. Arduino Pro Mini: commonly referred to as 5v/16MHz. Key features:

- Operating voltage level: 5.0 volts

- Speed of the Clock: 16 MHz

- Number of Digital input/output terminals: 14

- Analog input terminals: 8

- Pulse-Width Modulation power: 6

- Programming Interface: FTDI (compatible header)

f. Arduino Pro Mini (3.3v/16MHz). Key features:

- Operating voltage level: 3.3 volts

- Speed of the Clock: 8 MHz

- Number of Digital input/output terminals: 14

- Analog input terminals: 8
- Pulse-Width Modulation power: 6
- Programming Interface: FTDI (compatible header)

g. Arduino Mini 05. Key features:

- Operating voltage level: 5.0 volts
- Speed of the Clock: 16 MHz
- Number of Digital input/output terminals: 14
- Analog input terminals: 8
- Pulse-Width Modulation power: 6
- Programming Interface: FTDI (compatible header)

h. Arduino Pro 5v/16MHz. Key features:

- Operating voltage level: 5.0 volts
- Speed of the Clock: 16 MHz
- Number of Digital input/output terminals: 14
- Analog input terminals: 6
- Pulse-Width Modulation power: 6
- Programming Interface: FTDI (compatible header)

i. Arduino Pro 3.3v/8MHz. Key features:

- Operating voltage level: 3.3 volts

- Speed of the Clock: 8 MHz

- Number of Digital input/output terminals: 14

- Analog input terminals: 6

- Pulse-Width Modulation power: 6

- Programming Interface: FTDI (compatible header)

j. Red Board. Key features:

- Operating voltage level: 5.0 volts

- Speed of the Clock: 16 MHz

- Number of Digital input/output terminals: 14

- Analog input terminals: 6

- Pulse-Width Modulation power: 6

- Programming Interface: FTDI (through USB)

k. Arduino Uno (R3 SMD). Key features:

- Operating voltage level: 5.0 volts

- Speed of the Clock: 16 MHz

- Number of Digital input/output terminals: 14

- Analog input terminals: 6

- Pulse-Width Modulation power: 6

- Programming Interface: USB (through ATMega16U2)

1. Arduino Uno R3. Key features:

- Operating voltage level: 5.0 volts

- Speed of the Clock: 16 MHz

- Number of Digital input/output terminals: 14

- Analog input terminals: 6

- Pulse-Width Modulation power: 6

- Programming Interface: USB (through ATMega16U2)

2. Arduino Board Types based on ATMEGA32u4 Microcontroller technology:

a. Arduino Leonardo

Features:

- Operating voltage level: 5.0 volts

- Speed of the Clock: 16 MHz

- Number of Digital input/output terminals: 20

- Analog input terminals: 12

- Pulse-Width Modulation power: 7

- Programming Interface: Native USB

b. Pro Micro 5v/16 MHz

Features:

- Operating voltage level: 5.0 volts

- Speed of the Clock: 16 MHz

- Number of Digital input/output terminals: 14

- Analog input terminals: 6

- Pulse-Width Modulation power: 6

- Programming Interface: Native USB

c. Pro Micro 3.3V/8 MHz

Features:

- Operating voltage level: 5.0 volts

- Speed of the Clock: 16 MHz

- Number of Digital input/output terminals: 14

- Analog input terminals: 6

- Pulse-Width Modulation power: 6

- Programming Interface: Native USB

d. LilyPad Arduino USB

Features:

- Operating voltage level: 5.0 volts

- Speed of the Clock: 16 MHz

- Number of Digital input/output terminals: 14

- Analog input terminals: 6

- Pulse-Width Modulation power: 6

- Programming Interface: Native USB

3. Arduino Board Types based on ATMEGA2560 Microcontroller technology:

a. Arduino Mega 2560 R3

Features:

- Operating voltage level: 5.0 volts

- Speed of the Clock: 16 MHz

- Number of Digital input/output terminals: 54

- Analog input terminals: 16

- Pulse-Width Modulation power: 14

- Programming Interface: USB through ATMega 16U2

b. Mega Pro 3.3V

Features:

- Operating voltage level: 3.3 volts

- Speed of the Clock: 8 MHz

- Number of Digital input/output terminals: 54

- Analog input terminals: 16

- Pulse-Width Modulation power: 14

- Programming Interface: FDI (Compatible header)

c. Mega Pro 5.0V

Features:

- Operating voltage level: 5.0 volts

- Speed of the Clock: 16 MHz

- Number of Digital input/output terminals: 54

- Analog input terminals: 16

- Pulse-Width Modulation power: 14

- Programming Interface: FDI (Compatible header)

d. Mega Pro Mini 3.3V

Features:

- Operating voltage level: 3.3 volts

- Speed of the Clock: 8 MHz

- Number of Digital input/output terminals: 54

- Analog input terminals: 16

- Pulse-Width Modulation power: 14

- Programming Interface: FDI (Compatible header)

Arduino Board Types based on AT91SAM3X8E Microcontroller technology:

a. Arduino Due. Key features:

- Operating voltage level: 3.3 volts

- Speed of the Clock: 84 MHz

- Number of Digital input/output terminals: 54

- Analog input terminals: 12

- Pulse-Width Modulation power: 12

- Programming Interface: USB native.

Chapter Review

The main points in this chapter are highlighted below:

Arduino is an open-end prototype platform that enables people to write and integrate codes into a physical board when prototyping.

Features of Arduino

- Most of the Arduino boards available in market are able to take in both digital and analog input signals.

- Most Arduino boards can be controlled remotely from a computer harboring an Arduino IDE (Integrated Development Environment).

- Most of the existing or previous programmable circuit boards require an external hardware commonly referred to as a programmer.

- Arduino IDE has been simplified and is user-friendly since one only requires basic knowledge on C++ programming language.

- Surely, the invention of Arduino is a great achievement as it breaks the more complex work of having to deal with micro-controllers.

Arduino Evolution

Arduino was introduced into the market by a group of Engineers under the umbrella of Banzi Massimo, an Italian citizen in the year 2005.

Types of Arduino Boards

Arduino Boards are classified according to:

1. Arduino Boards based on ATMEGA328 microcontroller technology

- ✓ LilyPad Arduino
- ✓ LilyPad Arduino 328
- ✓ Arduino Fio
- ✓ Arduino Ethernet
- ✓ Arduino Pro Mini
- ✓ Arduino Pro Mini (3.3v/16MHz).
- ✓ Arduino Mini 05.
- ✓ Arduino Pro 5v/16MHz.
- ✓ Arduino Pro 3.3v/8MHz.
- ✓ Red Board.
- ✓ Arduino Uno (R3 SMD). Key features:
- ✓ Arduino Uno R3.

2. Arduino Board Types based on ATMEGA32u4 Microcontroller technology:

- ✓ Arduino Leonardo
- ✓ Pro Micro 5v/16 MHz
- ✓ Pro Micro 3.3V/8 MHz
- ✓ LilyPad Arduino USB

3. Arduino Board Types based on ATMEGA2560 Microcontroller technology:

✓ Arduino Mega 2560 R3

✓ Mega Pro 3.3V

✓ Mega Pro 5.0V

✓ Mega Pro Mini 3.3V

4. Arduino Board Types based on AT91SAM3X8E Microcontroller technology:

Arduino Due (latest version and fastest board in currently in the market)

Assessment

1. Clearly define the term Arduino?

2. What is does IDE means in full? Give its significance with regards to Arduino programming.

3. Name the father of Arduino

4. Explain various classifications of Arduino boards giving examples in each case

5. Why is Arduino Due referred to as the fastest Arduino board? Substantiate your claims.

Chapter 2

ARDUINO COMPONENTS

Chapter Objectives

The learners are expected to perform the following at the end of this chapter:

1. By the end of this chapter, the learner should be able to:

2. Clearly label all the parts of Arduino Uno board.

3. Explain the functions of each part of Arduino Uno board.

4. Explain power supply system of Arduino Uno board.

5. Relate a breadboard to Arduino programming

6. Highlight the tools used in Arduino circuit development

Arduino Board Breakdown

Arduino Uno remains to be the most common and used Arduino board in the world. This is because, Arduino Uno board has a simplified package and easy to understand parts clearly outstanding from one another. Again this explains why it is the most documented board in the market. Some boards may look different from Arduino Uno but the most necessary features are common to all the boards. These components are shown in the diagram below:

The parts that make up Arduino Uno board are defined below:

1. **Reset Button:** This is a button used to restart any string of codes that has been loaded to the Arduino board. Arduino Uno can be reset in two ways. First by pressing the button labeled 1. Secondly, connecting the Arduino board to an external reset button through the Arduino pin labeled RESET next to the Arduino pin labeled 12.

2. **Analog reference** (AREF): This button is used specifically to set an external voltage that lies between 0 to 5 volts depending on the type of Arduino board.

3. **Ground Pin (Pin labeled 14):** An Arduino board always has a number of ground pins which all can be used to ground the circuit. Grounding is a safety precaution to protect the circuit and the user as well.

4. **Digital Input/Output pin:** Normally Arduino board Uno has a total of 14 digital I/O pins ranging from pin 0-13. Six of these pins provide PMW (Pulse-Width Modulation technique) output. The rest can be configured to accept logic values (0 or 1) as inputs. Also the pins can also be used to drive differential modules (accept digital outputs as there inputs) including relays and LEDs.

5. **PWM:** There is one pin labeled "~" which can be used to generate Pulse-Width-Modulation signals which are analog in nature.

6. **USB:** Most Arduino boards can be powered easily from a computer through the USB cable. You only need to connect the USB cable from your computer unto the USB Connection pin. This kind of connection may also be used to upload sketches to the Arduino kit.

7. **LEDs TX and RX:** normally on the Arduino board there are two pins labeled TX to mean transmit and RX meaning transmit. These are the only two kind of pins that simultaneously appear at two different places on the Arduino board. First on the digital pins labeled 1 ad 0 where they are responsible for serial communication. The other TX and RX appear on the pin labeled 7 where TX is used for sending data while RX is used primarily for receiving data. The flashing speed of the LED on the TX depends on the baud rate (number of symbols or signal transmitted per second). RX on the other side flashes only when the board is receiving data. Therefore, these are indicators of transmission and reception activities with an Arduino board.

8. **AT mega controller:** This is the brain of the board though different Arduino boards have their own different controllers. It is an Integrated Circuit usually manufactured by the ATMEL Company. This where all the processing activities take place after the codes have been loaded therein. You must ascertain the type and features of your IC before loading codes for execution. All these information about the Arduino board IC is readily available on top of the IC. More information about the details and functions of the IC can be obtained from the data sheet given during purchase or obtained online from ATMEL Company website.

9. **Power LED indicator:** When the Arduino board is plugged into a power source through the USB port, this LED should light as an indication that the board has been successfully powered and in the right manner. The LED does not light whenever there is a fault with power connection.

10. **Voltage Regulator:** This is a crucial component of the Arduino Board that functions to control the amount of voltage into the board and also stabilizers the DC voltage to levels usable by the processor and other Board elements.

11. **Barrel Jack DC Power:** When there is no USB power supply, this port can be used as an alternative power supply from an external DC source.

12. **12 and 13. (3.3v and 5.0v):** these ports supply 3.3v and 5.0v respectively used to power your various projects.

13. **Analog Pins:** When the board is connected to an analog signal source like analog sensors, it is through these pins that the

board obtains such signals and converts them into digital before execution by the processor.

Power Supply

Arduino Board like any other electronic needs power to be able to operate. There are a number of ways to power Arduino Uno but most people prefer using the USB cable. The cable is connected directly to a laptop or a computer that supplies regulated 3.3v or 5.0v as per the requirement of your board. Again, there is the option of a battery pack of 9V. This enhances the portability of your project and the ability to operate even within remote areas. The last option would be to operate on a 9V AC power supply from a regulator that could be more expensive as compared to other power sources.

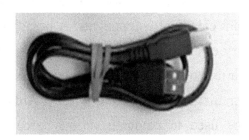

USB Cable

9V AC power supply adapter

9V DC battery pack

Breadboard

When working with Arduino board, it is necessary to use a solderless breadboard. This is a special board consisting of tie points or holes in which there are metal clips for conduction. Connection from each metal clip is completed by strips of conductive materials most likely copper.

The copper strips are laid horizontally implying that there is continuous connection horizontally. Any connection in the vertical way can be done using jumper wires to complete the circuits. Most breadboards can be used successfully as a motherboard where all the components of a project are mounted and the circuit powered remotely. The jumper wires also enables one to form circuits by inserting other components like resistors, capacitors, buzzers, LEDs, switches and many other relevant electrical components. A breadboard enables one to create temporary circuits different at time, easy to manipulate and come up with a variety of designs. This is possible since one does not to solder the circuit together. Apart from Arduino projects, a breadboard can be used to navigate various circuit designs during project fabrication.

Tools Needed for Arduino Projects

Apart from the Arduino board and breadboard, there are many other numerous tools necessary for soldering and completing the circuit. For beginners, I would strongly recommend just a soldering gun and a solder wire. These would be the most preferable tools for startup. Nonetheless, the other major tools are highlighted below which can be readily obtained in the market.

Soldering iron

One cannot do that much with the soldering gun minus the soldering iron or rod. This is the tool you will need to solder various components like a resistor in Arduino board. Components like LEDs need to be connected to the board using a soldering gun. At times, this tool is used to do the reverse of soldering. Components which did not auger well on the Arduino board, faulty components and needless components need to be removed from the board through a process of disordering. This tool uses AC power, 240 volts to operate though with a low power consumption.

Soldering gun

Wire Cutter

This is among the most used tools during soldering process because you have to resize, reshape and rewire different types of connecting wires from one component to another. There are other components like capacitors, diodes and resistors that always come with long legs that need to be resized. In this case, wire cutter would be the most appropriate tool to use. Again connecting wires need to be striped so as to connect effectively o the board. The process of removing the insulator requires the use of a wire cutter.

Solder Sucker

Just as the name suggests, this is a tool used primarily to remove or suck the solder away from the solder joint. It is basically a pump that works by the principle of creating a low pressure zone inside it allowing the solder to rise upwards from the joint or board. When you need to remove the solder professionally, first of all heat the solder joint to form a solder liquid. Then use this tool to suck it off immediately. Normally big companies that use machine soldering apply the same principle to remove a lot of solder with a lot of ease and also at once. Another good tool to perform this particular task would be a solder wick. This is a unique machine made of copper threads that easily absorb the solder from the solder joint. Give it a try someday and you will have the best results. You do not have to struggle to remove solder bits between various chips on a board. Sometimes, the solder left on the joint may be too little that sing a pump may prove futile. Therefore using a solder wick would be the best option.

Tweezers

This is like a safe handle during soldering process. Normally the soldering gun is always heated to high temperatures roughly 100° Celsius therefore when you use your hands you will definitely burn. To keep you safe during this process, you need to use a pair of tweezers that helps in holding components as you align them to their right positions. Tweezers can access even very small positions where the human hand cannot be able to get in. When doing a crucial process called surface mount where small components are mounted on the board you will definitely use a pair of tweezers.

Pair of tweezers

Wet Sponge

As the name suggests, this is wet surface of sponge used basically to clean the tip of the soldering gun. When used for a long time, the soldering gun tend to acquire some impurities and dirt due to induction that in the end will reduce the effectiveness of the soldering process. The soldering gun is therefore cleaned regularly by placing the tip in the wet sponge. The tip always oxidize very fast and therefore form a layer that will reduce the rate of heat transfer. To solder well, the soldering gun tip should be hot enough to effectively melt the solder.

Safety Glasses

Soldering is more like a welding process though on a small scale therefore protective gear is necessary. To start is the safety glasses, accidentally some pieces of solder may splash into the eye due to negligence hence it is necessary to wear this protective equipment. Most people doing soldering always assume this crucial protection scheme, but wait until you get into trouble. So to look like a scientist, give it a try.

Mask

When doing soldering, the melting solder always produces a gas that is poisonous when inhaled. Most of the soldering rods or iron are made up of lead as one of the key components, burning lead produces a gas that can cause serious respiratory problems when inhaled for a long time. This is why human soldering is not recommended on large scale. One can do this kind of job for a short while then rotate to another department. Fortunately, there are machines already in the market that can perform soldering more precisely. Before soldering, make sure you have clad yourself in a mask for your own personal safety.

Soldering Mat

Finally you need a mat to keep all your components intact, also to reduce the time needed to pick the components from different places. This mat is made up a heat resistant material and therefore cannot easily burn. The various compartments are helpful in keeping electronic components while disassembling and repairing an electronic appliance.

Anyone aspiring to begin serious soldering processes relating to Arduino must count the cost first then consider to purchase the following items commonly called Arduino kit startup:

- Arduino Uno

- USB cable

- A book of at least 15 projects

- A breadboard

- Connecting wires

- Wooden base

- Battery pack 9V

- Phototransistor 6x

- Potentiometer 3x

- Pushbuttons 10x

- Sensors (TMP36)

- LEDs of different colors

- Transistors, capacitors and resistors

Chapter Review

Arduino Uno remains to be the most common and used Arduino board in the world

The key parts that make up Arduino Uno board are:

- ❖ Reset Button

- ❖ Analog reference (AREF)

- ❖ Ground Pin

- ❖ Digital Input/Output pin

- ❖ PWM

- ❖ USB

- ❖ LEDs TX and RX

- ❖ AT mega controller

- ❖ Power LED indicator

- ❖ Voltage Regulator

- ❖ Barrel Jack DC Power

- ❖ Analog Pin

Breadboard

This is a special board consisting of tie points or holes in which there are metal clips for conduction. Connection from each metal clip is completed by strips of conductive materials most likely copper.

Power Supply:

- USB Cable

- 9V AC power supply adapter

- 9V DC battery pack

Tools Needed for Arduino Projects:

- Soldering iron

- Wire Cutter

- Solder Sucker

- Tweezers

- Wet Sponge

- Safety Glasses

- Mask

- Soldering Mat

Assessment

1. Draw and labeled clearly all the parts of Arduino Uno.

2. Explain the functions of the following parts of an Arduino Uno.

    a. Reset Button

    b. Analog reference (AREF)

    c. Ground Pin

d. Digital Input/Output pin

e. PWM

f. USB

g. LEDs TX and RX

h. AT mega controller

i. Power LED indicator

j. Voltage Regulator

k. Barrel Jack DC Power

l. Analog Pin

3. Explain the process of desoldering during circuit design.

4. What are the power options of an Arduino Uno? Describe each and every source highlighting their advantages and disadvantages.

5. Describe the key feature of the soldering mat including why it is used during soldering.

Chapter 3

GETTING STARTED WITH ARDUINO

Chapter Objectives

The learners are expected to perform the following at the end of this chapter:

1. Clearly describe the Arduino platform

2. Highlight and explain the Arduino hardware specifications

3. Explain the features of the Arduino software (IDE)

4. Describe the stages and all processes involved in the installation of Arduino on your computer

5. Describe the process of installing Arduino drivers on Macintosh

6. Describe the process of installing Arduino on Windows Operating system.

7. Be able to describe and identify the various ports of Arduino in Macintosh

8. Be able to describe and identify the various ports of Arduino in Windows Operating System

The Arduino Platform

Arduino as mentioned earlier is composed of two major parts, that is, the Arduino board and the Arduino IDE. Arduino board is the piece of hardware where the circuit developer works on during the design and implementation of a project. It is on this board that various electronic components are mounted, tested than run to realize specific objectives. Not one time can Arduino programming be undertaken without this board? In fact the name Arduino first originated with the use of the board, this what was in the mind of the father of Arduino.

Arduino IDE (Integrated Development Environment) is another key feature that must exist in your computer for you control the Arduino project mounted on the Arduino board. So you only need to create some codes or rather programs on this IDE then load them to Arduino in which they get executed by the processor and the result is displayed as desired. Therefore it is necessary that one installs this software in their personal computers. The IDE is very crucial even in the design of electronic circuits. Imagine changing the whole components of an electronic project. It is very expensive to change even the capacitors of a circuit already mounted on the board. Think about even having to desolder a resistor from the Arduino board. It is more expensive and time consuming than having just to change the codes on your computer.

One may desire to change the resistance of a specific circuit, just by the touch of a button, it is very possible to navigate through all these technicalities. Even changing the direction of current flow is possible through the IDE. This is therefore a program that all those who desire to use Arduino must learn how to install, manipulate its settings and even connect to the Arduino board. This is what this chapter will cover in fine details right from basics to a bit complicated stuff. Are you ready for the flight into the world of Arduino? Cover yourself because you are about to get into that section of the book that is most interesting and engaging. Be sure to perform a lot of downloading and installation processes on your personal computer.

Getting Started with the Arduino Hardware

As mentioned earlier, the Arduino hardware comprises primarily of microcontroller board with various components and ports for integrating the whole circuit during implementation. Nothing is interesting as to learn how to connect various parts of your circuit into the Arduino board. Of course for power purposes, the USB port is there to help in case you are using your personal computer to power the Arduino. For external power source e.g. battery pack of 9 volts, there is a port to allow connect your power source.

This is also true for an AC 9 volts power source. So once you have confirmed that your Arduino is working properly as indicated by the LED power indicator that immediately lights when the board is powered. You can disconnect our board from the power source to avoid being electrocuted then begin to mount your various components one by one. Make sure to confirm that each and every component is mounted at the right port and section. Ensure external devices like sensors are connected on the right ports so as to give the right results. Some devices are meant to give analog signals unto the board while other ports are supposed to transfer the digital output from the board to an external device e.g. a motor.

Arduino Software Environment

The IDE (Integrated Development Environment) basically implies a very special program designed specifically for Arduino users. This is where all the control functions of Arduino board take place through sketches basically in the processing language that is easy to understand and manipulate at the same time. Over 7 billion people of this globe are expected to use this software with a lot of ease and therefore it is a platform that is very basic in its functionality. A statement like "light diode A' is quickly transformed into a language familiar to Arduino board and is quickly executed by the processor and the diode A lights when all other pertaining factors are kept constant and perfect. This kind of magic requires a close connection between the IDE and the Arduino board. So what happens with the sketches until the Arduino reacts accordingly? Check out on the next paragraph.

The IDEs of the earlier times enabled one to write sketches on the platform that would be later transformed into machine language by a special program called a compiler. Another special program called an interpreter comes in between the sketches and the programming languages like C++ or Java. The interpreter works in hand with the compiler to ensure that the sketches are transformed into a language that the Arduino board can understand. Nowadays there are IDE platforms that allow one to write codes directly in a high level language like C++, C, C#, Java and many other languages. This kind improvement is necessary due to the ever improving technology and the need to bridge the gap between software and hardware. It is very true that Arduino makes life very easy for circuit designers since most of the complexities are softly handled behind the scenes. Arduino also alleviates the whole process of having to program a microcontroller that definitely will take ages together with more than enough errors. The Arduino IDE even has self-mechanism of handling errors a process commonly referred to as troubleshooting.

Programs on Arduino IDE can edited, deleted, copied and even printed for documentation purposes. Assume you have developed and designed a very wonderful electrical project that need to be well documented, you have the option of printing your codes from the IDE and even procedures. This makes Arduino more friendly interface. The simple life cycle of Arduino program consists of:

❖ Put on the Personal Computer if it is the source of power for your Arduino board. In case you are using a different power source, plug in it unto the Arduino board ensuring that you use the right port. Using a USB cable, connect your Arduino board on to the personal Computer. This is just to power the board ready to accept commands rom the IDE.

❖ Simply write a rough sketch on the IDE platform, this sketch should aim at bringing the board to life as we shall learn more later.

❖ Upload this sketch using the USB cable to the Arduino board and keep calm for magic to happen so that the board restarts.

❖ Finally the board executes your sketches through the processor (an Integrated Circuit on the Arduino Board). The board should restart if indeed the sketches were right. In case of any errors, IDE should return an error message and possible suggest solutions that can help solve the problems with your sketches.

It is equally important to highlight the fact that there are other IDEs for other softwares like Java Programming. This simply implies that

Arduino IDE should never be mistaken to function for other programs. This is specifically meant to serve purposes of Arduino programming with inbuilt features dedicated to Arduino board. Other software IDEs will not necessarily work in the programming of an Arduino board. There are key features that are dedicated to a specific software that should never be mistaken. The processors themselves are very different in many aspects like: speed, power requirement, memory use, deadlock handling and many other key areas.

Yes there are similar components existing among these IDEs like programming languages used. Mostly nowadays, programming languages used in these IDEs include: C, C++, Java, Python, C# plus many others. These are the most commonly used languages due to the ease of writing, editing and execution. Again most of them have been incorporated into the curriculum of most learning institutions or one may decide to pursue these courses on online classes where certification is guaranteed.

The Arduino board uses its processor to execute various codes or sketches using the clock technology. The number of cycles of the processor makes in a second determines its speed normally expresses in Hertz, Megahertz or even Gigahertz. Currently most Arduino board have a speed of 84 Megahertz (84 MHz) meaning that the processor can make 84 million turnarounds in just one second. This is incredible and a satisfactory speed, ability of the Arduino board to handle as many codes as possible within a very short time frame. With this trend, future Arduino boards will be very minute but very powerful able to handle a lot of task with increased precision. With the introduction of robots, most of the prototyping would be done remotely hence enhancing processing capability while reducing the workload on the user side. Who knows what the future has for Arduino programming.

Arduino Installation Procedure

Arduino is an open-ended software which can be accessed and downloaded by anyone provided you having a stable network together with an updated search engine. As stated earlier, one must first of all download the Arduino IDE software before being able to program the Arduino board. Currently, there are several sites available from which the software can be accessed easily. To download Arduino IDE follow these simple steps:

I.   First of all establish a secure and stable internet connection through a mobile hotspot, Wi-Fi connection or Wi-Fi connection.

II. Then open your favorite browser, that is, Google Chrome, Mozilla Firefox, Microsoft Edge or Windows Explorer then on the search button type the words "Arduino IDE download" then press Enter key.

III. On your computer, the browser will bring a number of options from the latest version from different developers. Be sure to choose the best option that which is compatible with your computer hardware and Operating system. I would prefer the latest version that is most likely to be very compatible with a number of new hardware and software. 2019 version would be the best option as for now with the latest updates and best quality in terms of its features.

IV. After selecting the latest version, double click on the link, it is always the title of that web page written in blue color. The link will then direct you to the website where you are supposed to download Arduino IDE. On the website, you will notice a number of tabs and links to various sites including the download link. Ignore all the ads since they may not be necessarily helpful at this very stage.

V.   Go direct to the download link, double click and wait for a more instructions. When using strong and fast networks, the link should open immediately and indicate to you that the download is in progress. However, you may be directed to wait a little bit so as to secure a stable connection. Be sure to note the folder where you will find the downloaded file immediately when it is done. Normally most downloaded files are sorted into a file named 'Download", this is the default setting of most Personal Computers using the current Operating systems like Windows 10.

Mostly the downloaded Arduino IDE file will come as a compressed file only manipulatable by WinRAR. Double click on the Compressed File, to open it up a process referred to us decompression.

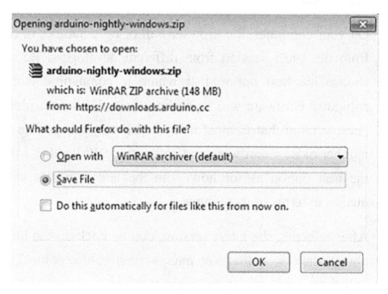

WinRAR file

By the end of this process you will be able to have a file named Arduino-[version], for example, Arduino-0019. You can now change the location of this folder to wherever folder that suits you best. I would prefer you create a folder named Arduino either on your desktop or within local disk G. You can now cut your Arduino-0019 file to this particular location. Wow! You are now ready to install Arduino IDE on your personal computer.

Installing Arduino Drivers on Macintosh

It is that good time you have been waiting for as to install Arduino IDE on your PC. The first installation will be for Macintosh operating System and therefore we must be able to determine the right Arduino drivers. Drivers are special programs within a software that helps creates a network between the software itself and the hardware of the computer. For example, when Arduino IDE wants to access computer microphone, it will use the drivers associated with microphone in order to bridge the gap.

Procedure for installation:

1. Go to the location where you had stored the folder Arduino and open the file Arduino-0019 by double-clicking on it.

2. Once you have opened this particular file, look for a specific file named FTDIUSBSerialDriver_x_x_x.dmg *where _x_x_x will be a combination of unique digits representing the version number of this particular driver. For example, 019 can be the version of* Arduino-0019 Macintosh driver.

3. The next step is to double-click on the FTDIUSBSerialDriver_x_x_x.dmg to begin the installation

process. Or you can also right-click on this particular file and select "Run as Administrator" option.

4. The next step will be to confirm this kind of installation. Once you mount the drive file, a checkbox will appear prompting you to confirm your installation. Be sure to confirm by clicking "OK".

5. The installation process will proceed slowly or fast enough depending on the processing power of your Personal Computer.

6. You should be in a position to follow all the instruction as per the installer, make sure you choose only those options that will not terminate the installation process. When asked for the password, please type the one for administrative user and you will be almost done with this installation.

7. When the installation process completes and you see a message "Arduino IDE has been installed successfully" or any other text relating to this, please restart your computer even if you are not prompted to do so. This is to ensure that the Operating System loads IDE drivers and sets them ready for use the next time you log into your computer.

8. Once the computer has restarted, double-click on the Arduino IDE icon to start the program and at the same time power your Arduino board by connecting it to the PC through the USB cable.

9. By this time, the powered board should be able to give indications of life. For example, the PWR indicator of the board should light while the yellow LED labeled "L" should also come on by blinking. This is an indication that the installation

process was very successful and the board is ready to receive commands from the IDE platform.

NOTE: In case your machine is an Intel-based Mac including, MacBook, MacBook Pro or iMac; please only install those drivers with the label "Intel". That is to mean, double click the driver that looks like this: FTDIUSBSerialDriver_x_x_xIntel.dmg. *For those machines which are not Intel-based, feel free to install the driver without "Intel" label on it.*

Installing Arduino Drivers on Windows

Windows currently is the dominating Operating System and most companies prefer this type of System software. Windows has been updating its features for all the available versions with Windows 10 currently used all over the globe. Other versions of windows include: Windows XP, Windows 7, Windows 8, and Windows 8.1 amongst others. This shows that developers of Arduino IDE must be able to keep track of windows updates so that they also can roll out compatible software. Windows is a special case of System software that allows one to either download versions of Arduino IDE which are compatible with various versions of windows from the internet. The other option would be to allow windows to update automatically Arduino IDE drivers once the software has been installed into your personal computer. This section will explore both options as a way to give yourself a variety of choices.

Installation Procedure

For the already installed Arduino software, you only need to allow the system software to automatically load the right drivers.

This process may require internet but can be done when drivers are already stored in a local disk. We will describe the procedure involving this whole process:

1. First of all you need to power the Arduino board through a connection to the personal computer using a USB cable.

2. Windows have automatic search power called New Hardware Wizard that pops up whenever the computer is connected to a new device. This wizard will help windows to search in the Windows update site for compatible drivers with the new hardware. For windows XP version, you will be prompted to check for Windows update.

3. Windows XP will update the required drivers when given a go ahead while other versions will update automatically. In the case of drivers not found or you select a "NO, not at this time" for windows XP, there is remains another option of updating these drivers from a local storage.

4. Once step 2 above fails, you can choose net step that will direct you to a screen that guides you through drivers' installation from disk.

5. Double-click on the tap "Install drivers from a local storage", then get direct to the specific location where you had downloaded Arduino IDE and select that particular folder.

6. After selecting the folder, windows automatically isolates these drivers from the list provided. Windows actually looks for the most compatible driver and the latest version.

7. After identifying the right folder, select OK and Next.

8. Once the updates are complete, your computer is ready to work with these new drivers. Only one steps remains, you need to restart your computer so that your PC may load these drivers and incorporate them into the system. During restart time, your PC loads the new drivers into its control panel where they are given rights to access your PC resources like processor, memory, input devices and output devices as well.

9. Windows Vista works in a similar manner with Windows XP these versions are becoming obsolete with time due to the production of upgraded hardware. This is why Windows Company is working hard in enrolling new features of windows so as to attract more customers and be able to remain competitive in the market.

NOTE: Sometimes while installing Arduino IDE in your computer, you may encounter compatibility issues where the drivers may not necessarily run on your computer. These upgrades can be done online where Windows can automatically identify the latest updates which are compatible with your Personal Computer. Again, Windows 10 latest version has an Update Assistant that automatically check new features of existing drivers whenever the computer is connected to an internet. These updates are installed in the background and when the computer restarts, they are loaded into the control panel. Sometimes the Personal Computer may prompt you to restart whenever these downloads are ready to be installed and incorporated as part of the system hardware.

Before working on your Arduino projects, it is very important to correctly identify ports with regards to the main Operating Systems, which are, Windows and Macintosh. This forms the bulk of work in our next section.

Arduino Ports on Macintosh

There are different ports on IDE platform that have been configured to work under different settings and therefore the user must select the best port for the right results.

On Macintosh platform, once you have launched the IDE there are various tabs on the status bar which are explained below:

1. **Arduino:** This gives the name of the platform you are using and most of the times its labeled Arduino to imply that your IDE is one that is developed specifically to be used on Arduino programming exclusively. Not any other software may be able to receive codes from Arduino IDE.

2. **File:** This is the tab that directs the user to a new project or an existing project. When double-clicked, a list of options appear like saving, creating new project, linking a project with an existing one plus many other available options. it is quite interesting to realize that Arduino files are always linked with one another, that is to mean a file can use the codes in another file successfully and also be able to share its codes.

3. **Edit:** This tab presents the user with a number of manipulation options while writing the codes. Errors can be deleted and corrections made appropriately.

4. **Tools:** These are inbuilt IDE tools to help in manipulating the various sketches and codes on the platform. This is also where communication settings are located. The settings are crucial in ensuring continuous data transfer with the Arduino board. So the port identification are done over here. So from this menu,

you are to select "Serial Port". Next from the options given, select the port that is looks like this "dev/cu.usbserial".*Typically this is the unique name that connects your computer with the Arduino board. So whenever your computer makes references to the board, IDE drivers will navigate the processor to that particular name.*

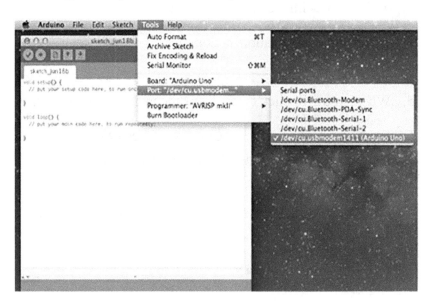

Port Identification on Macintosh

Arduino Ports on Windows

For windows Operating System, the Process of Port identification is quite complicated especially at the beginning. Anyway, guide thyself as we explore this wonderful procedure.

The procedure goes:

1. Click on the Start Menu at the Taskbar, on the search field, type "Device Manager" and click "Ok". The device manager appears as a list of various hardware components of your

45

computer. In fact you can be bale to notice the various drivers installed in your Personal Computer.

2. Once on Device Manager, right-click on Ports (COM & LPT) then a list will appear.

3. From the list available on Port (COM & LPT), Arduino port will appear with the label USB Serial Port (COM).

4. Once this configuration is complete, you will get back to the IDE platform.

5. Where you will click on the tools menu that to serial port.

6. From the serial port, you can now choose that particular port name that you just figured from the Device manager. And the process is complete.

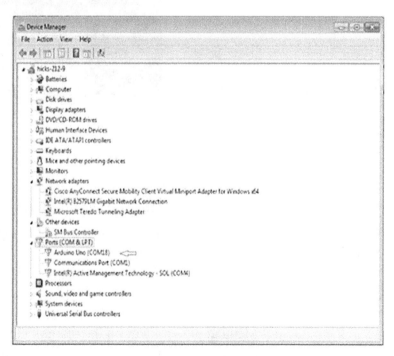

Port identification in windows

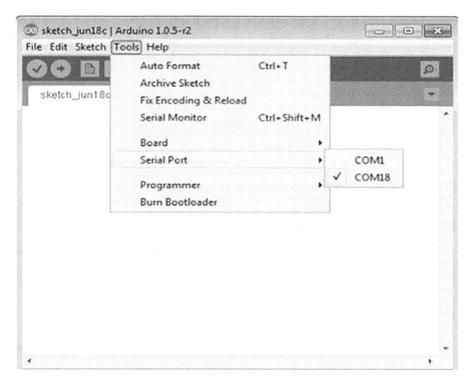

Port identification in windows

Arduino IDE Toolbar

When you launch Arduino IDE, like any other program it presents an interactive platform with an easy to use window. This window also has a toolbar containing various tabs which are discussed below:

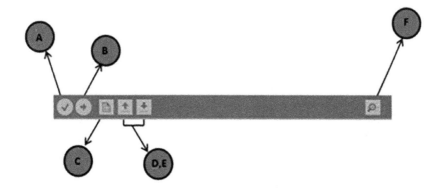

A. This tab is used to for compilation errors in the codes and sketches.

B. The tab is used when uploading new programs to the Arduino board.

C. When you want to create a new sketch or codes, simply use this shortcut tab.

D. A tab used to open an already existing sketch

E. Saving tab after doing all your work then you need to click this button in order to save. Ensure you save your work before loading them to the Arduino board.

F- A tab known as a Serial Monitor responsible for sending and receiving of data to and from the Arduino board.

> ➢ After writing the sketches or your codes and saving, click on the "Upload" tab on the platform. After a few seconds, the TX and RX LEDs o the Arduino board will begin to flash. For successful loading, you should be able to see a message "Done Uploading" appear in the status.

> ➢ For Arduino Mini and NG, the operator needs to press physically the "Reset" button just before uploading your sketches to the board.

Chapter Review

The Arduino Platform

Arduino board is the piece of hardware where the circuit developer works on during the design and implementation of a project. Arduino IDE (Integrated Development Environment) is another key feature that must exist in your computer for you control the Arduino project mounted on the Arduino board.

Getting Started with the Arduino Hardware

The Arduino hardware comprises primarily of microcontroller board with various components and ports for integrating the whole circuit during implementation.

Arduino Software Environment

The IDE (Integrated Development Environment) basically implies a very special program designed specifically for Arduino users.

The life cycle of Arduino program consists of:

- Put on the Personal Computer if it is the source of power for your Arduino board. In case you are using a different power source, plug in it unto the Arduino board ensuring that you use the right port. Using a USB cable, connect your Arduino board on to the personal Computer.

- Simply write a rough sketch on the IDE platform, this sketch should aim at bringing the board to life.

- Upload this sketch using the USB cable to the Arduino board and keep calm for magic to happen so that the board restarts.

- Finally the board executes your sketches through the processor (an Integrated Circuit on the Arduino Board).

Arduino Installation Procedure

Simple steps to download Arduino IDE:

- First of all establish a secure and stable internet connection through a mobile hotspot, Wi-Fi connection or Wi-Fi connection.

- Type the words "Arduino IDE download" on your favorite browser then press Enter key.

- On your computer, the browser will bring a number of options from the latest version from different developers. Be sure to choose the best option that which is compatible with your computer hardware and Operating system.

- After selecting the latest version, double click on the link, it is always the title of that web page written in blue color.

- Go direct to the download link, double click and wait for a more instructions.

Installing Arduino Drivers on Macintosh

Go to the location where you had stored the folder Arduino and open the file Arduino-0019 by double-clicking on it. The next step is to double-click on the FTDIUSBSerialDriver_x_x_x.dmg *to begin the installation process. Or you can also right-click on this particular file and select "Run as Administrator" option.*

Installing Arduino Drivers on Windows

Windows is a special case of System software that allows one to either download versions of Arduino IDE which are compatible with various versions of windows from the internet. The other option would be to allow windows to update automatically Arduino IDE drivers once the software has been installed into your personal computer

Arduino Ports on Macintosh

From the Tool's menu, you are to select "Serial Port". Next from the options given, select the port that is looks like this "dev/cu.usbserial".*Typically this is the unique name that connects your computer with the Arduino board. So whenever your computer makes references to the board, IDE drivers will navigate the processor to that particular name.*

Arduino Ports on Windows

From the Device manager menu configure the right port name from the Ports (COM & LPT) option and choose this particular name on "Tools" menu on the IDE platform.

Assessment

01. What is the function of the Arduino board in the design and implementation of Arduino projects?

02. What do we call the process of ensuring there continuous communication between Arduino IDE and Arduino board?

03. Installing Arduino IDE on Windows platform is possible through two different methods. Highlight these methods giving advantages and disadvantages of each method.

04. When downloading Arduino IDE on Windows, there are factors to consider. Explain three of these factors describing results of non-compliance to them.

05. Arduino IDE status bar has various tabs. Name these tabs while giving their specific functions.

06. Describe the process of port identification with Windows Operating System.

Chapter 4

INTRODUCTION TO ARDUINO PROGRAMMING

Chapter Objectives

1. At the end of this chapter, the learner should be able to:

2. Describe the structure of an Arduino program

3. Explain the various data types of Arduino programs

4. Describe the various variable and constants of Arduino program

5. Clearly describe control statements associated with Arduino programming giving examples.

6. Define Arduino programming functions, string and arrays

7. Explain Arduino time with respect to Arduino programming

Arduino Programming-Structure

This chapter will delve much into Arduino program structure with new terminologies being explained. Arduino programming is based on Java programming under the GPL together with C and C++ programming languages. All these are a sub-section of LGPL. Just like any other programming environment, Arduino IDE borrows a lot from C and C++ libraries.

The first term under this section is the "Sketch" which is a collection of codes that are aimed to accomplish a specific function on the Arduino board. The codes are written in a language familiar to the IDE, for example, C++ then translated into machine language before execution by the processor of the Arduino Board. An Arduino program is composed of three major parts, that is: Structure, values and functions. Values are either variables or constants. For this section we will learn about these parts of an Arduino program stepwise until we get to learn how to write programs from scratch to complex stuff. So to begin, we shall tackle **Structure**: consist mainly of two parts;

- Setup ( ) function

- Loop ( ) function

For example in a program:

```
void setup ( )
{
}
```

Function: This is part of a code is only invoked/recalled during the initialization of a sketch. The IDE platform runs this section when the sketch starts. Some of its major uses may include: initialization of variables, used when invoking pin modes, during the start of libraries and e.t.c.

This function only runs once immediately after powering the Arduino board or when you restart the board remotely or by physically pressing the restart button. It has three parts, that is, **input, output** and **return** as we will discuss later.

```
void loop ( )
{
}
```

This is the part of a sketch that comes immediately after the setup ( ) has done all the initialization processes. As the name suggests, it is involved with consecutive looping allowing you to change and respond appropriately. The codes can automatically do this whenever this part of a sketch is invoked. Precisely, it is a crucial section used to actively control the Arduino board. Just like the setup ( ), loop ( ) also has three parts namely: Input, output and return.

Arduino Data Types

Data types as explained in C programming refers to those extensive ways used to declare variables and functions at different points. Data types are crucial section in any programming since the length and type determines the amount of storage they will occupy in the memory. Apart from storage, the interpretation of bits of these data types are equally important. Nothing has become so precious like storage that is why even in programming, we are careful of the amount of space our codes will occupy. The aim is to use the least possible storage since technology is evolving into microchips with great processing and storage capabilities.

The data types that we will cover in Arduino programming are listed below:

Void, Boolean, char, unsigned char, byte, int, unsigned int, word, long, unsigned long, float, double, String-char array, array and String-object.

Void

This is a keyword always used with those sections of the code to indicate that the function is not expected to return any information to that particular function. Mainly used during function declaration as shown below:

```
void loop ( )

{

          // the other codes

}
```

Boolean

The name is derived from an ancient Scientist called Boolean, this data type holds only one values among two, that is, either true or false. They are variables that only occupy one byte of memory.

For example:

```
boolean val = true ;    // variable declared with data
type Boolean then initialized

//to with true.

boolean state = false ; // variable declared with data
type Boolean then initialized

//to with true.
```

Char

Char is a shortened character, therefore implies a data type that occupies only one byte of the memory while storing a character value. Character values can be literals written as single quotes, eg. 'B' or

"CBA" for multiple characters. Double quotes are used with multiple characters while single quotes are for a single character. Characters again are stored as numbers according to ASCII chart with each character assigned a specific value for example, 'A'-65. It is therefore possible to perform Arithmetic operations with characters, e.g. 'A' + 2 has the value 67.

Example is a program:

```
Char chr_b = 'b'; // variable declared with data type
char then initialized

//With a character b

Char chr_a = 100; // variable declared with data type
char then initialized

//with a character 100
```

Unsigned char

This is an unsigned data type as the name suggests, occupies one byte in the memory like normal char data type. Unsigned data type is used to represent numbers from 0 to 225.

Example in a program:

```
Unsigned Char chr_x = 99; // variable declared with
data type unsigned char then

//initialized with a character x
```

Byte

This is an 8-bit data type that is able to store unsigned numbers of 8 bits from 0 to 225.

Example in a program:

```
Byte n = 100; // variable declared with data type byte
then

//initialized with 25
```

Int

Int (Integers) basically are the primary data types used to store numbers. And integer stores a 16-bit value that is, two bytes combined together. On the minimum side, char can store up to -2^{15} (-32768) while on the maximum end the values should not exceed $(2^{15}-1)$ = (32767). This indeed a wide range of values.

Different Arduino boards have varying int sizes, for example, Arduino Due is able to accommodate 32-bit int size (4-byte value). The range lies between -2^{31} (-2,147,483,648) and $(2^{31}-1) = (2,147,483,647)$.

Example in a program

```
Int counter = 20; // variable declared with data type
int then

//initialized with 20
```

Unsigned int

Unsigned int refers to unsigned integers are more less the same as int data type with an exception of being able to store only positive numbers. The range in this case lies from 0 to 65,535 that is $(2^{16}-1)$. For Arduino board Due, it is bale to tolerate double unsigned int. The range therefore would be from 0 to 4,294,967,295 $(2^{32}-1)$.

Example in a program

```
Unsigned int counter = 19; // variable declared with
data type unsigned int then

//initialized with 19
```

Word

ATMEGA based boards like Arduino Uno, a word is a 16-bit value consisting of unsigned number. However on Arduino board Zero and Due, a word stores a 32-bit value of unsigned number.

Example in a program:

```
Word q = 145; // variable declared with data type word
then

//initialized with 145
```

Long

These are extended size variables in order to store numbers, 32 bits (4 bytes) with a range of 2,147,483,648 to 2,147,483,647.

Example in a program:

```
Long speed = 18; // variable declared with data type
long then

//initialized with 18
```

Unsigned long

These are extended size variables in order to store numbers, 32 bits (4 bytes). However, unsigned long data types can only store positive numbers with a range of 0 to 4,294,967,295 equivalent to (2^{32} - 1).

Example in a program:

```
Unsigned Long acceleration = 108; // variable declared
with data type long then

//initialized with 108
```

Short

This is a 16-bit data types (2-byte) producing a range from -32,768 to 32,767. The minimum is at -2^{15} and the maximum value at 2^{15}.

Example in a program:

```
Short val = 8; // variable declared with data type
short then

//initialized with 8
```

Float

Also referred to as floating-point data type implying a number with a decimal point. Floating-point numbers are preferred over integers since they have a higher resolution which is an important aspect when approximating analog and continuous values.

Examples of floating-point numbers would be 3.125469702A+25 and 2.2645126987E+38. These numbers can store 32 bits of information (4 bytes).

Example in a program:

```
float num = 5.23658; // variable declared with data
type float then

//initialized with 5.23658
```

Double

Double on Arduino Uno and other ATMEGA boards implies those data types that are floating-point precision and occupies a memory space of four bytes. Its implementation is more or less as that of a float apart from the fact that there is no gain in precision. However on other Arduino boards like Arduino Due, double data type occupies a memory space of 8 bytes, that is, 64 bits precision.

Example in a program

```
double num = 35.23658; // variable declared with data
type double then

//initialized with 35.23658
```

Arduino Variables and Constants

Right, before we begin looking at Arduino variables and constants, it is equally important to understand one crucial point. We shall explain the concept of variable scope.

Variable scope

This is a concept in C programming language implored in Arduino programming where within the variables there exists a property known as scope. A scope in simple terms is a specific region in a program and normally there are different regions where a variable can be declared. These are:

♦ Within a function or inside a block of functions and this scope is known as local variables.

♦ The region can as well exist in the definition section of a function parameter.

♦ The variables can be declared right outside of all the blocks and blocks.

1. Local Variables

As stated earlier, these are variables that are declared right inside the functions or within a group of functions commonly known as a block. These variables are useful only to those statements which lie inside the functions or inside the blocks. Local variables however do not function on their own but require the assistance of the statements and blocks.

Example in a program:

```
Void setup ()
{
 }
Void loop ()
{
int a , b ;
int c ; // declaration of a Local variable
a= 0;
b=0;     //initialization of a local variable
c=10;
}
```

Global Variables

These are those variables that have been declared outside the functions and blocks especially at the top of a particular program. After declaration, local variables are able to hold their values all the throughout the life time of your program. Again once declared, local variables are accessible to any other function all through the entire program. That means, they can be recalled by statements written before or after they have been declared.

Example in a program:

```
Int R, T;
float d =1;          // declaration of Global variable
Void setup ()
{

}
Void loop ()
{
int a , b ;
int c ;              // declaration of Local variable
a= 0;
b=0;                 //initialization of local variables
c=10;
}
```

Arduino Operators

An Arduino operator is that particular symbol that is used specifically to instruct the compiler to perform a particular arithmetic, mathematical and logical operation. C language has a number of operators that enable circuit designers to include mathematical operations in their circuits.

These operators include:

- ❖ Compound Operators

- ❖ Comparison Operators

- ❖ Boolean Operators

- ❖ Bitwise Operators

- ❖ Arithmetic Operators

We will begin our discussion with the most basic operators.

Arithmetic Operators

We will use an example to explain these operators that is to mean, we will assume variable X holds a value of 10 while variable Y holds a value of 20. Arithmetic operators are explained below:

01. Assignment Operator (=): This operator means that the value on the right of the equal sign will be stored in the variable that will be to the left of the equal sign.

Example: Y=X

02. Addition (+): This operator adds two operands separated by the addition sign. Example: X+Y gives a result of 30

03. Subtraction (-): The operator subtracts the second operand (variable on its right) from the operand on its left. Example X-Y gives a result of 10.

04. Multiplication (*): This operator multiplies both operands on its sides. Example: X*Y gives a result of 200

05. Division (/): The operator divides the numerator by the denominator. Example: X/Y gives a result of 2

06. Modulo (%): This operator is also called a Modulus operator that gives the remainder of an integer after a division operation.

Example: X%Y gives a result of 0

Example in a program:

```
void loop ()
  {
      int x=9,y=4,z;
      c=x+y;
      c=x-y;

      c=x*y;
      c=x/y;
      c=x%y;

  }
```

Results:

x+y =13

x-y =5

x*y=36

x/y=2

Remainder when x is divided by y =1

Comparison Operators

As the name suggests, these are operators used to compare the values of two or more variables depending on the specifications stated. Here we will assume that variable X holds a value of 10 while variable Y holds a value of 20.

01. **Equal to (==):** This function is supposed to check if the values of two variables or operand are equal. If it is so, the condition becomes true and if not, the condition is false. Example: (X==Y) the result is false or not true.

02. **Not equal to (!=):** This operator is meant to check whether the values of two operands or variables are equal or not.

The condition becomes true when the values of the two operands or variables are not equal. Example: (X!=Y) the result is true.

03. **Less than (<):** This operator is meant to check if the value of the left variable f operand is less than the value of the operand on the right side. If this condition is fulfilled, then the result becomes true. Example: (X<Y) the result is true.

04. **Greater then (>):** This operator is meant to check if the value of the left variable f operand is greater than the value of the operand on the right side. If this condition is fulfilled, then the result becomes true. Example: (X>Y) the result is false or not true.

05. **Less than or equal to (<=):** This operator is meant to check if the value of the left variable f operand is less than or equal to the value of the operand on the right side. If this condition is fulfilled, then the result becomes true. Example: (X<=Y) the result is true.

06. **Greater than or equal to (>=):** This operator is meant to check if the value of the left variable f operand is greater than or equal to the value of the operand on the right side. If this condition is fulfilled, then the result becomes true. Example: (X>=Y) the result is not true or false.

Example in a program:

```
void loop ()
{
        int x=9,y=4
        bool z = false;
if(x==y)
```

```
        z=true;
  else
      z=false;


  if(x!=y)
            z=true;
  else
          z=false;
  if(x<y)
        z=true;
  else
        z=false;


  if(x>y)
            z=true;
  else
          z=false;
  if(x<=y)
      z=true;
  else
              z=false;
  if(x>=y)
              z=true;
  else
              z=false;
  }
```

Results

z=false

z=true

z= false

z=true

z= false

z= false

Boolean Operators

We will explain these operators using examples where we will assume that the variable X holds a value of 10 while a variable Y holds a value of 20.

01. And (&&): This operator is referred to as the Logical And. It gives a result of true when the operands on both sides are non-zero. Example: (X&&Y) the result is true.

02. Or (||): This operator is referred to as the Logical Or. It gives a result of true when either the values of the operands on any of the sides is non-zero. Example: (X||Y) the result is true.

03. Not (!): This operator is referred to as the Logical Not. It is used specifically to reverse the logical condition of the operands on both sides. Example :!(X&&Y) the result is false.

Example in a program:

```
void loop ()
{
    int x=9,y=4
    bool z = false;
        if((x>y)&& (y<x))
        z=true;
        else
        z=false;
    if((x==y)|| (y<x))
```

```
        z=true;
        else
        z=false;
if(  !(x==y)&& (y<x))
        z=true;
        else
        z=false;
}
```

Results:

Z=true

Z=true

Z=true

Bitwise operator

We will explain these operators using examples where we will assume that the variable X holds a value of 10 while a variable Y holds a value of 20.

> **01. And (&):** This operator is commonly known as the Binary And Operator meant to copy a bit and gives the results in binary form if the bits exists in both the operands. Example: (X&Y) the result is 12 which in binary form is written as 00001100
>
> **02. Or (|):** This operator is commonly known as the Binary Or Operator meant to copy a bit and gives the results in binary form if the bits exists in both the operands. Example: (X|Y) the result is 61 which in binary form is written as 00111101.

69

03. Xor (^): This operator is commonly known as the Binary Xor Operator meant to copy a bit and gives the results in binary form if the bits exists only in one operand but not both the operands. Example: (X^Y) the result is 49 which in binary form is written as 00110001.

04. Not (~): This operator is commonly known as the Binary Ones Complement Operator meant to flip bit and is unary in nature. Example: (~X) the result is -60 which in binary form is written as 11000011.

05. Shift left (<<): This operator is commonly known as the Binary Left Shift Operator meant shift the value of operand on the left to the left side by a specific number of bits always specified by the value on the right and gives the results in binary form if the bits exists in the operands. Example: (X<<2) the result is 240 which in binary form is written as 11110000.

06. Shift right (>>): This operator is commonly known as the Binary Right Shift Operator meant shift the value of operand on the left to the right side by a specific number of bits always specified by the value on the right and gives the results in binary form if the bits exists in the operands. Example: (X<<2) the result is 15 which in binary form is written as 00001111.

Example in a program:

```
void loop ()
{
int x=10,y=20
```

```
int z = 0;
    z= x & y ;
    z= x | y ;
    z= x ^ y ;
    z= x ~ y ;
    z= x << y ;
    z= x >> y ;

}
```

Results

z=12

z=61

z= 49

z=-60

z=240

z=15

Compound Operators

We will explain these operators using examples where we will assume that the variable X holds a value of 10 while a variable Y holds a value of 20.

01. Increment Operator (++): This operator is supposed to increase the integer by a value of one whenever the code is invoked. Example: X++ gives a result of 11.

02. Decrement Operator (--): This operator is supposed to decrease the integer by a value of one whenever the code is invoked. Example: X-- gives a result of 9.

03. Compound Addition (+=): This operator is also known as Add AND assignment operator used to add the value of the right operand to the value of the left operand and the result is assigned to the left operand. Example: Y+=X gives a result of Y=Y+X.

04. **Compound subtraction (-=):** This operator is also known as Subtract AND assignment operator used to subtracts the value of the right operand from the value of the left operand and the result is assigned to the left operand. Example: Y-=X gives a result of Y=Y-X.

05. **Compound multiplication (*=):** This operator is also known as multiply AND assignment operator used to multiply the value of the right operand with the value of the left operand and the result is assigned to the left operand. Example: Y*=X gives a result of Y=Y*X.

06. **Compound division (/=):** This operator is also known as Divide AND assignment operator used to divide the value of the right operand with the value of the left operand and the result is assigned to the left operand. Example: Y/=X gives a result of Y=Y/X.

07. **Compound modulo (%=):** This operator is also known as Modulus AND assignment operator used to take the modulus of the value of the right operand and the value of the left operand and the result is assigned to the left operand. Example: Y%=X gives a result of Y=Y%X.

08. **Compound bitwise or (|=):** This operator is also known as bitwise inclusive OR together with assignment operator. Example: X|=2 gives a result of X=X|2.

09. Compound bitwise and (&=): This operator is also known as bitwise AND together with assignment operator. Example: X&=2 gives a result of X=X&2.

Example in a program:

```
void loop ()
{
  int x=10,y=20
  int z = 0;
     x++;
     x--;
     y+=x;
     y-=x;
     y*=x;
     y/=x;
     x%=y;
     x|=y;
     x&=y;
}
```

Results

x=11

x=9

y=30

y=10

y=200

y=2

x=0

x=61

x=12

Chapter review

- Arduino Programming-Structure:

  01. Setup ( ) function

  02. Loop ( ) function

- Arduino Data Types:

  01. Void

  02. Boolean

  03. Char

  04. Unsigned char

  05. Byte

  06. Int

  07. Unsigned int

  08. Word

  09. Long

  10. Unsigned long

  11. Short

  12. Float

  13. Double

➤ Arduino Variables and Constants:

01. Within a function or inside a block of functions and this scope is known as local variables.

02. The region can as well exist in the definition section of a function parameter.

03. The variables can be declared right outside of all the blocks and blocks are called global variables.

➤ Arduino Operators:

❖ Arithmetic Operators:

01. Addition (+)

02. Subtraction (-)

03. Multiplication (*)

04. Division (/)

05. Modulo (%)

❖ Comparison Operators

01. Equal to (==)

02. Not equal to (!=)

03. Less than (<)

04. Greater then (>)

05. Less than or equal to (<=)

06. Greater than or equal to (>=)

- ❖ Boolean Operators

  01. And (&&)

  02. Or (||)

  03. Not (!)

- ❖ Bitwise operators

  01. And (&)

  02. Or (|)

  03. Xor (^)

  04. Not (~)

  05. Shift left (<<)

  06. Shift right (>>)

- ❖ Compound Operators

  01. Increment Operator (++)

  02. Decrement Operator (--)

  03. Compound Addition (+=)

  04. Compound subtraction (-=)

  05. Compound multiplication (*=)

  06. Compound division (/=)

  07. Compound modulo (%=)

  08. Compound bitwise or (|=)

  09. Compound bitwise and (&=)

Assessment

01. What is meant by the term Arduino programming structure?

02. Using simple programs, differentiate between set up ( ) function and loop ( ) function.

03. Give the range of values which can be stored by the following data types:

a) Void

b) Boolean

c) Char

d) Unsigned char

e) Byte

f) Int

g) Unsigned int

h) Word

i) Long

j) Unsigned long

k) Short

l) Float

m) Double

04. Give the essential difference between the following data types:

a) Char

b) Unsigned char

c) Int

d) Unsigned int

e) Long

f) Unsigned long

05. Define the term variable scope with reference to Arduino programming variables.

06. Explain the difference between local variables and global variables.

07. Give the functions of the following Arduino operators:

a) Multiplication (*)

b) Not equal to (!=)

c) Less than (<)

d) Greater than or equal to (>=)

e) Or (||)

f) Xor (^)

g) Shift right (>>)

h) Decrement Operator (--)

i) Compound subtraction (-=)

j) Compound division (/=)

k) Compound bitwise or (|=)

08. What is the key difference between the following Arduino operators?

    i.   Addition (+) and Compound Addition (+=)

    ii.   Subtraction (-) and Compound subtraction (-=)

    iii.   Multiplication (*) and Compound multiplication (*=)

    iv.   Division (/) and Compound division (/=)

    v.   Modulo (%) and Compound modulo (%=)

    vi.   Compound bitwise or (|=) and Compound bitwise and (&=)

Chapter 5

ARDUINO PROGRAMMING TOOLS

Chapter Objectives

By the end of this chapter, the learner should be able to:

❖ Explain Arduino Control Statements as applied in Arduino programming

❖ Using examples describe the various functions used in Arduino programming

❖ Explain the types of string as a components of Arduino programs

❖ Expound on Arduino time constrains with practical examples

❖ Illustrate with examples arrays applied in programming of Arduino IDE

Arduino Control Statements

Control structures involved in decision making demand that the person doing the actual programming (programmer) clarifies and specifies certain conditions that will be tested and evaluated by the program itself. These condition should be written along with some statements that will be executed if the condition is to return a value. Otherwise, other statements will be executed so as to return a false response or outcome for the condition.

Most of the programming languages have a general format for decision making structures as illustrated below:

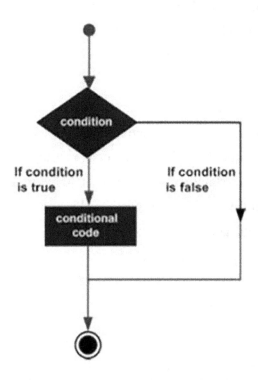

The statements within the control structure (condition) as mean to coordinate the flow of program execution and are therefore referred to as Source Code Control Statements.

These are statements include:

    If statement

    If….else statement

    If…else if…else statement

    Switch case statement

    Conditional operator?

Again just to emphasize, these statements are very important in navigating through various loops and sections in a program. Executing one part at a time and using the results to instruct the processor on the next block of codes to be executed.

If statement

This particular structure uses expressions in parenthesis together with statements or block of statements in the next line of codes. When the expression is true, then the processor is instructed to execute the block of statements or statements that were included in this condition. And if the expression is false, the processor skips the block of statements or statements and gets to the next line of codes. If statement takes two kinds of forms as explained below:

First form

```
{

if (expression)
block of statements;

}
```

Second form

```
if (expression)


{

statements;

}
```

Execution Sequence of If Statement

The order of execution for if statement is summarized below by the diagram:

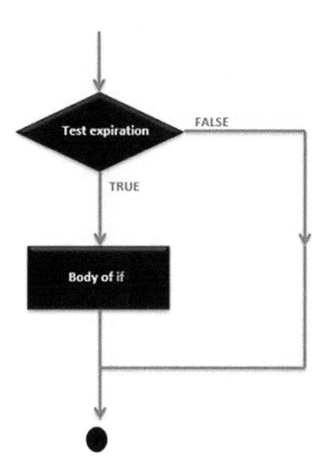

Example in a program:

```
/* definition of Global variables */
int X = 5 ;
int Y= 9 ;
Void setup ()
{
```

```
}
Void loop ()
{
/* this section is used to check the boolean condition
*/
    if (X > Y) /* when the condition is true then the
processor is to execute the

    statement below*/
    Y++;
/* this part is use to check the boolean condition */
    If ( ( X>Y ) && ( Y!=0 )) /* when this condition is
true then the processor executes the statement below*/

    {
        X+=Y;
      Y--;
    }
}
```

The If...else statement

This structure provides an alternative statement to be executed in case the condition is false, that is to mean when if statement is false, then there is an optional way out since there is a provision of an optional else statement to be executed.

<u>Syntax</u>

```
if (expression)
{
    statements;  //these statements are executed only
when the condition is true
}
else
```

```
{
    statements; // optional statements to be executed
in case the expression is false.
}
```

Summary of the execution sequence

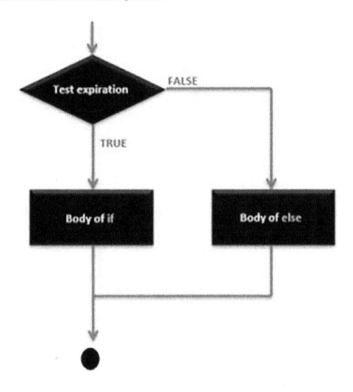

Example in a program

```
/* definition of Global variables */
int X = 6 ;
int Y= 8 ;
Void setup ()
{

}
Void loop ()
{
```

```
/* this section is used to check the boolean condition
*/
    if (X > Y) /* when the condition is true then the
processor is to execute the

    statement below*/
    {

        X++;
        }

    else

        {

            Y-=X

        }

}
```

If...else if...else statement

This is a special control structure where an if statement is followed by an optional else..if...else control structure. Such an expression is quite important in navigating through conditions to test whether they are true or false.

NOTE: Always remember the following points while using If...else if...else statement:

It is possible for an **if statement** to have none or just one else statement, and the if statement must always come after any else if's.

It is lawful for an **if statement** to have none or many else if statements that must always come before the else statement.

All else if or else statements succeeded by an else if will never be executed since the processor goes by a mode of priority.

<u>Syntax</u>

```
if (first expression)
  {
     statements or block of statements;
  }
else if(second expression)
  {
     statements or block of statements;
}
.                  //other else if statements

.

.

.
else
  {
statements or block of statements;
  }
Example in a program
/* definition of Global variables */
int X = 5 ;
int Y= 9 ;
int Z=15;
Void setup ()
{
}
Void loop ()
{
    /* checks if the boolean condition below is true or
```

```
false */
    if (X > Y)   /* when the condition is true the
processor is instructed to execute the statements
below*/

{
        X++;
    }
    /* checks if the boolean condition below is true or
    false */
    else if ((X==Y )||( Y < Z) ) /* when the condition is
    true the processor is instructed to execute the
    statements below */
        {
          Z=Y* X;
    }
    else
        Z++;
}
```

Switch Case Statement

This kind of control structure works in a similar manner with if statements where the programmer is able to specify the different levels of codes that will be executed for different conditions.

A **switch** statement is instructed to compare the value of some variables against the specified values written within the **case** statement hence the name switch case. So the processor looks for a case statement with similar value to that of the switch statement then executes the codes in that particular case statement.

A **break** statement is used at the end of each case statement to enable the execution to exit at the end of each case. Without a break, execution will go through a state called **falling-through** where the switch statement will go on running the following until that point when there will a break or typically at the end of the switch statement.

Syntax

```
switch (variable)
{
        name of the case:
        // statements or block of statements
                break;
    }
        name of case:
        {
        // statements or block of statements
                break;
        }
    default case:
        {
        // statements or block of statements
                break;

        }
    }
```

Example in a program:

We will use a very simple example where we will assume a variable with only three states, that is, high, low and mid representing logic levels of 0, 1 and 2. The program is supposed to switch the code according to the right routine. The codes would therefore look like this:

```
switch (variable state)
{
        case 0: Low();
```

```
        break;
    case 1: Mid();
        break;
    case 2: High();
        break;


    default case:
    Display ("Invalid state!");
}
```

Conditional Operator?

Conditional operator remains to be the only ternary operator in Arduino programming as well as in C programming language.

<u>Syntax</u>

First expression? second expression: third expression

Explanation: The first expression is executed first then depending on the outcome of this first execution, the subsequent expressions are either processed or skipped. That is to mean, when the outcome of expression is true, then the second one is executed and the sequence continues. When the first expression gives a false result then the execution skips expression two and processes expression three. Expression should give a result of either true or false depending on the condition to be satisfied.

Example in a program:

```
/* Find min(x, y): */
min = ( x > y ) ? x : y;
/* this portion is supposed to Convert a small letter
to a capital: */
/* (parentheses may not necessarily be required in this
case) */
z = ( z >= 'x' && x <= 'c' ) ? ( z - 45 ) : z;
```

Some of the rules to take care of while working with condition operator:

> ➤ Always ensure that the first expression is of a scalar type.

> ➤ For the subsequent expressions, keep in mind the following:

- ▪ If they are two, then both must be of arithmetic type

- ▪ If they are two, then both should be evaluated by simple arithmetic conversions which   eventually will determine the resulting type.

- ▪ If they are two, they should both use the void set up giving a result which is void in nature.

Arduino Programming Loops

Programming loops are more or less like control structures that provide for more complicated paths for execution.

Therefore a loop statement makes a provision for the execution to process statements or a block of statements in a multiple of times. The general schematic diagram is shown below:

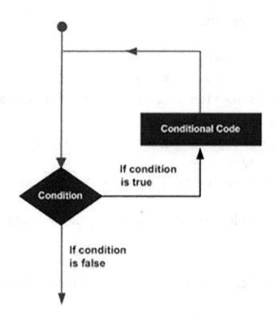

Arduino programming together with C language provides the following types of loops:

- While loop

- Do…while loop

- For loop

- Nested loop

- Infinite loop

While Loop

This loop continues to execute or process infinitely until that point in time when the expression inside the parenthesis gives a false result. Actually while loop will never exit unless something changes with the nested variables.

```
while(expression)
  {
statements or block of statements;
  }
```

Do...while loop

Do...while loop is similar to while loop only that in while loop execution, the condition for loop-continuation is tested right at the commencement of loop before execution gets to the body of the loop. While in do...while loop, execution tests the body of the loop before checking the condition for loop-continuation.

After execution of a do...while loop execution (after termination), execution actually goes on to process those statements after the while statement.

Syntax

```
Do

{

     Statements or block of statements;

}

  while (expression);
```

For loop

For this kind of a loop, the statements are executed for a predetermined number of successions. Within the for loop expression, the control expression is initialized, tested and changed during execution.

This presents a very easy to debug arrangement where the structure has a looping behavior which is entirely independent of the activities happening inside the loop.

For loop has three expressions inside the parenthesis which controls its operation. The expressions are separated by with semicolons.

<u>Syntax</u>

```
for ( expression initialization; control part;
increment or decrement portion)
   {
        // statements or block of statements
   }
```

Example in a program:

```
for(counter=3;counter >=10;counter++)
   {
      //statements or block of statements will be
executed 10 times
   }
```

Nested Loop

This is a technique where you can use a loop inside another loop as illustrated below by the syntax.

<u>Syntax</u>

```
for (expression initialization ;control part; increment
or decrement portion)
    {
         // statements or a block of statements
  for (expression initialization ;control part;
increment or decrement portion)
```

```
    {
        // statements or a block of statements
    }
}
```

Example in a program:

```
for(counter=0;counter<=10;counter++)
 {
   //statements or a block of statements will be
executed 10 times
   for(j=0;j<=100;j++)
    {
        //statements or a block of statements will be
executed 101 times
    }
 }
```

Infinite Loop

As the name suggests, this is a loop without a point of termination therefore executes infinite number of times.

<u>Syntax</u>

```
1. When using for loop

for (;;)
 {
   // statements or a block of statements
 }

2. Using while loop

while(expression)
  {
```

```
    // statements or a block of statements
  }
```

3. Using do...while loop

```
Do

  {
   Statements or a Block of statements;
  }

while(expression);
```

Arduino Functions

These are statements per see that allow programmers to structure their programs in parts or segments that are meant to perform particular tasks at a time. For example, a function would be helpful when one wants to perform a particular task a multiple times in a program.

Advantages of code segmentation into standardized fragments:

∇ Segmented codes presents a more organized work enhancing easier conceptualization such codes.

∇ During modification, code fragments are least liable to error since any mistake is easily noticeable.

∇ Codes stay compact and there is reduced space since most of the codes are reused several times.

∇ Functions presents a modular set up of codes that is easy to read and can be reused in other sections.

Arduino programming provides for two compulsory functions, that is, set up ( ) and loop ( ). Other functions must be created right outside of the brackets of the above functions.

Common syntax defining a function:

```
Return   type   function   name   (first   argument,   second
argument,  …..)

        {

                Statements or a block of statements

        }
```

Explanation:

o   Return type: the type of value that is returned by the function, for example, any data type.

o   Function name: Identifier or title by which this function can be recalled.

o   First argument, second argument…: These are parameters that are used to define the data type.

o   Statements or a block of statements: Incorporates the statements or the body of the function itself.

Function Declaration

Any function is supposed to be declared outside other functions, that is, below or above loop ( ) function.

Function declaration can take two forms namely:

∇ Just writing the function prototype just above the loop ( ) function and this form consists of: Return type, name, and argument type. Function prototype is always followed by a semi-colon.

<u>Example in a program:</u>

```
int aver_func (int a, int b) // declaration of the
efunction
{
  int c=0;
    c= a+b ;
    return z; // return the result's value
}
void setup ()

{
    Statements // block of statements
}
Void loop ()
{
  int result =0 ;
    result = Aver_func (8,7) ; // part of the program
referred to as a function call
}
```

∇ The function declaration part or function definition is declared below the loop ( ) function and consists of: Return type, name and argument type.

Example in a program:

```
int aver_func (int , int ) ; // part of the program
called a function prototype
void setup ()
{
    Statements //    block of statements
}
Void loop ()
{
  int result =0 ;
      result = Aver_func (9,10) ; // part of the
program called a function call
}
int Aver_func (int a, int b) // declaration of this
function
{
      int b=0;
      b= a+c ;
      return b; // return the resultant value of b
}
```

Arduino Programming- Strings

Strings are used purposely to store texts and can be use sometimes to display the stored texts on an LCD or Arduino IDE Monitor window. User inputs can also be stored using strings.

The two types of strings used in Arduino programming are:

o Character arrays which are equivalent to strings in C programming language

o Arduino String that enables programmers to use a string object as part the sketch.

So in this chapter we will be able to identify strings, objects and which types of strings to use in Arduino programming (sketches).

String of Character Arrays

This is typically a series of characters of the data type char also called an array consisting char variables. An array therefore would mean a collection texts of the same data type and stored in a memory.

However a string is a special type of array with an extra element always zero at the end of it.

Example in a program:

```
void setup()
{
    char go_str[7]; // an array which can accommodate
string made up of six characters
    Serial.begin(10000);
    go_str[0] = 'G'; // this string is made up of six
characters
    go_str[1] = 'o';
    go_str[2] = 'o';
    go_str[3] = 'd';
    go_str[4] = 'i';

    go_str[5] = 'e';
    go_str[6] = 0; // the 7th array element called a
null terminator
    Serial.println(go_str);
}
void loop()
{

}
```

This same example can be rewritten in a more convenient way as shown below:

```
void setup()
{
    char go_str[] = "Goddie";
    Serial.begin(10000);
    Serial.println(go_str);
}
void loop()
{

}
```

Before this string is executed, the compiler is supposed to calculate its size and automatically terminate it using the null terminator.

Manipulation of a String Array:

We will consider the sketch below to explain how to manipulate a string array.

```
void setup()
{
 char take[] = "I do not take mangoes and tea"; //
creating a string array
    Serial.begin(10000);
        // the codes below are used to print the
string
    Serial.println(take);
        // the codes below are used to delete part of
the string
    take[13] = 0;
    Serial.println(take);
        // the codes below explain how to substitute a
```

```
text into an existing string
    take[13] = ' '; // the null terminator replaced
with a space
    take[18] = 'e'; // point to insert the next new
word
    take[19] = 'g';
    take[20] = 'g';

    take[21] = 0; // null terminator used to terminate
the string
    Serial.println(take);
}
void loop()
 {
}
```

Result

✓ I do not take mangoes and tea

✓ I do not take mangoes

✓ I do not take mangoes and egg

Explanation

First you need to create and print a string. For the sketch above, a new string was created and displayed on the Serial Monitor window.

The second process is to shorten the string using a null terminator. That means when printing the new string, characters are displayed up to that point where there is the null terminator.

The next procedure is to change a word in a string. Firstly you have to replace the new null terminator with a space so that the string is restored to its original format. The next step is to replace the individual characters in the word to be replaced, that is, t-e-a with e-g-g.

The next example explains the various C programming string functions used to manipulate array strings:

```
void setup()
{
  char str[] = "This strings is ours"; // this section
creates a string
  char out_str[40]; // describes where the output from
string functions is placed
  int num;            // an integer for general purpose
  Serial.begin(10000);
                  // the codes blow are used to print
the string
  Serial.println(str);
                  // codes used calculate the string
length excluding the null     terminator
  num = strlen(str);
  Serial.print("Length of String is: ");
  Serial.println(num);
                  // codes used calculate the array length
including null terminator
  num = sizeof(str); // for this part note that
sizeof() is not part of C string function
  Serial.print("Array size: ");
  Serial.println(num);
              // codes for coping a string
  strcpy(out_str, str);
  Serial.println(out_str);
              // codes for adding a string to another a
string process called append
  strcat(out_str, " codes.");
```

```
        Serial.println(out_str);
        num = strlen(out_str);
        Serial.print("Length of String is: ");
        Serial.println(num);

        num = sizeof(out_str);
        Serial.print("Array size is out_str[]: ");
        Serial.println(num);
    }
    void loop()
    {

    }
```

Results

> This string is ours
>
> String length is: 16
>
> Array size is: 19
>
> This string is ours
>
> String length is: 22
>
> Array size out_str[ ]: 38

Arrays Bounds

Arrays and strings have specified bounds that restrict programmers to always work within those restrictions. In the above example, we created an array of 38 characters long and therefore trying to copy and array which is longer that this may be difficult. The copied longer array will be copied over the end of the created array.

Arduino Programming- Time

Arduino programming has a total of four time manipulation functions as listed below:

- Delay ( ) function

- Delaymicroseconds ( ) function

- Millis ( ) function

- Micros ( ) function

We will discuss each of these time functions and highlight their importance in Arduino programming.

Delay ( ) function

This presents the simplest time manipulation function among the four functions. Only a single integer is used as its input or argument. This integer represents a waiting time in milliseconds that instructs the program to wait until it moves on to the next group of codes where it will encounter the delay ( ) function.

Usually this function is not recommended to instruct your code to wait as it is associated with a phenomenon called "blocking".

Syntax

delay (ms) ; //ms represents delay tie in milliseconds normally associated with unsigned long

Example in a program:

```
/* Lighting LED
 * ------------
 * the code is meant to control the turning on and off
of an LED that has been connected to the digital pin,
with an interval of 2 seconds. *
*/
int LEDPin = 14; // the LED is connected to digital pin
number 14
void setup() {
    pinMode(LEDPin, OUTPUT); // digital pin is set as
the output
}
void loop()
{
    digitalWrite(LEDPin, HIGH); // the LED is set on
    delay(1000); // LED set to waits for half a second
    digitalWrite(LEDPin, LOW); // the LED is set to off
mode
    delay(500); // the LED is set to wait for half a
second

}
```

DelayMicroseconds ( ) function

Just lie the delay ( ) function, delayMicroseconds ( ) also accepts only a single integer as its argument or input. The integer here represents time in microseconds which is equivalent to a thousandth of a millisecond or a millionth of a second in this case.

Record time that has been tested and proved to be able to produce an accurate delay is 16383 which is subject to change depending on future inventions in Arduino boards' production. However, for delays less than thousand microseconds, it is advisable to use the delay ( ) function.

<u>Syntax</u>

delayMicroseconds (us) ; // the us represents the number of microseconds set for delay/pause usually taking unsigned int

Example in a program

```
/* Lighting an LED
 * ------------
 * the code is meant to control the turning on and off
of an LED that has been connected to the digital pin,
with an interval of 1 seconds. *
*/
int LEDPin = 14; // the LED is connected to digital pin
number 14
void setup() {
   pinMode(LEDPin, OUTPUT); // digital pin is set as
the output
}
void loop()
{
  digitalWrite(LEDPin, HIGH); // the LED is set on
  delay(500); // LED set to waits for half a second
  digitalWrite(LEDPin, LOW); // the LED is set to off
mode
  delay(500); // the LED is set to wait for half a
second

}
```

Millis ( ) function

The time delay used here is milliseconds, which is to mean, immediately the Arduino board runs a program, it returns a number of milliseconds. This delay time at times goes back to zero a phenomenon called "overflowing" after around 50 or so days.

Syntax

millis () ; // this function returns milliseconds from when the program begins.

Example in a program:

```
unsigned double delay time;
void setup(){
   Serial.begin(9600);
}
   void loop()
{
  Serial.print("delay time:");
  delay time = millis();
       //the codes below will print  time since the
program begun
  Serial.println(delay time);
       //this code dictate that you will have to wait
for a second to prevent sending //massive amounts of
data
delay time(1000);
  }
```

Micros ( ) function

This function also returns the amount of time from the beginning of the program, the time is expressed in microseconds. Overflowing phenomenon also happens here after a period of about 70 minutes.

Syntax

micros () ; // the function is supposed to return a time period in microseconds after the program ahs begun.

Example in a program

```
unsigned double delay time;
void setup(){
   Serial.begin(9600);
}
void loop(){
   Serial.print("delay Time:");
delay time = micros();
        //the codes below prints time period   since
program begun

   Serial.println(delay time);
        // this code dictate that you will have to wait
   for a second to prevent //sending massive amounts of
   data
   delay time(1000);

}
```

Arduino programming- Arrays

An array is a consecutive collection of elements of the same data type located in consecutive memory locations.

In locating a particular element in array, we must specify its name and the name of its storage location. Therefore an array has two important features, that is, name and location. Identifying an array is done by giving that particular element a name then by the element's position in a square bracket [ ]. The first element (called zero element) has a subscript zero and the subsequent elements can be represented by C[1], C[2], C[3] and the rest as shown in the figure below:

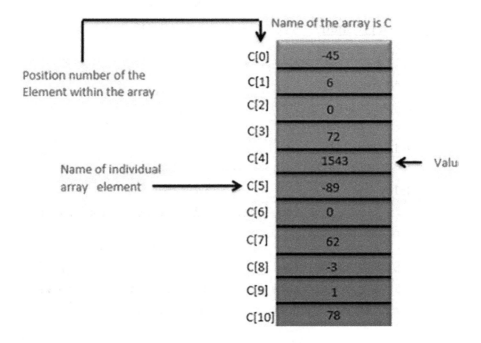

The above array is called C with 11 elements. Each element has a value for example C[10] has a value of 78.

We can therefore write programs to manipulate these values, for example, to print the sum of the values of the first three elements in the array we can write:

```
Serial.print (C[ 0 ] + C[ 1 ] + C[ 2 ] );
```

Again we can write another program to multiply the value of C[8] by 6 and assign the result to a variable called y:

```
x = C[ 8 ] * 6;
```

Arrays Declaration

Arrays declaration helps to specify the type of element and the total number of elements in that array as illustrated below:

```
type arrayName [ arraySize ] ;
```

This instructs the compiler to reserve enough memory for the array. That is why the array size must be an integer. For example:

```
int D[32]; // array name is D with an array size of 32
integers
```

Examples of programs using Arrays

Array declaration and then using a loop in the initialization of the array elements:

```
int b[ 12 ] ; // array name is b with 12 integers as
array size
void setup ()

{ }
void loop ()
{
   for ( int j = 0; j < 10; ++j ) // array
initialization with elements
   {
       b[ j ] = 0; // this codes sets element at location
j to be 0
       Serial.print (j) ;
       Serial.print ('\r') ;
```

111

```
}
    for ( int i = 0; j=i < 10; ++i ) // specifies the
output of each array element's //value
{
    Serial.print (n[i]) ;
    Serial.print ('\r') ;
}

}
```

Array declaration and initialization using an initializer list:

```
// b is an array made up of 12 integers
int b[ 10 ] = { 23, 20, 48, 12, 16, 28, 87, 79, 69, 37,
58,17 } ;
void setup ()

{

}
void loop ()
{
    for ( int j = 0; j < 10; ++j ) // the codes are used
for initialization of elements //in the array from n to
0
{
    Serial.print (j) ;
    Serial.print ('\r') ;
}
    for ( int i = 0; i < 10; ++i ) //codes that specify
the output of each array //element's value
{
    Serial.print (n[i]) ;
    Serial.print ('\r') ;
}

}
```

Multidimensional Arrays

An array of two dimensions mostly represent a table of elements consisting of rows and columns.

Some of the outstanding features of a multidimensional array:

- Has two subscripts representing the columns and rows of a table.

- The first subscript represent the elements' rows and the second subscript represents the elements' columns.

- Multidimensional arrays have two and more dimensions.

An example by declaration is shown below:

```
int c[ 3 ][ 3 ] = { { 3, 8 }, { 3, 7 } };
or int c[ 3 ][ 3 ] = { { 3 }, { 3, 9 } };
```

Summing all the Array elements

Those elements in an array normally represent values that are as a result of a calculation or those yet to be used in a particular math work. For example a professor may decide to enter the marks of students in a table forming an array then using the total to calculate the average marks of the class. The example below explains how this can be achieved using array functions.

const int arraySize = 5; // array size indicated by a variable called const and data type used is int

```
int c[ arraySize ] = { 80, 60, 50, 100, 70,};
int total = 0;
```

```
   void setup ()
{

}
   void loop ()
{
// the code below is used to get the sum of the
contents of array c
for ( int j = 0; j < arraySize; ++j )
    total += c[ j ];
Serial.print (" sum Total of elements of array c : ") ;
Serial.print(total) ;
}
```

Chapter Review

- ➢ Arduino Control Statements

  - ✳ If statement

  - ✳ If….else statement

  - ✳ If…else if…else statement

  - ✳ Switch case statement

  - ✳ Conditional operator?.

- ➢ Arduino Programming Loops

  - ✳ While loop

  - ✳ Do…while loop

  - ✳ For loop

  - ✳ Nested loop

  - ✳ Infinite loop

- ➢ Arduino Functions

  - ✳ Common syntax defining a function:

Return type function name (first argument, second argument, …..)

```
    {

         Statements or a block of statements

    }
```

* Parts

  o Return type: the type of value that is returned by the function, for example, any data type.

  o Function name: Identifier or title by which this function can be recalled.

  o First argument, second argument…: These are parameters that are used to define the data type.

  o Statements or a block of statements: Incorporates the statements or the body of the function itself.

* Function Declaration

  ➢ Arduino Programming- Strings

Strings are used purposely to store texts and can be use sometimes to display the stored texts on an LCD or Arduino IDE Monitor window

  ➢ Arrays Bounds

* Arrays and strings have specified bounds that restrict programmers to always work within those restrictions

  ➢ Arduino Programming- Time

    * Delay ( ) function

    * Delaymicroseconds ( ) function

    * Millis ( ) function

    * Micros ( ) function

➤ Arduino programming- Arrays

An array is a consecutive collection of elements of the same data type located in consecutive memory locations.

✳ Arrays Declaration

```
type arrayName [ arraySize ]
```

✳ Multidimensional Arrays

An array of two dimensions mostly represent a table of elements consisting of rows and columns.

Assessment

01. What are Arduino control statements and explain their function.

02. Using syntax representation, highlight the difference between the following control structures:

a) If statement and If....else statement

b) If...else if...else statement and Switch case statement

03. What makes Conditional operator a unique control statement?

04. Write a program illustrating the use of If...else if...else statement.

05. What is the need of programming loops in Arduino IDE?

06. Explain how While loop differs from Do...while loop.

07. Using syntax explain how nested loop is applied in Arduino programming.

08. Write a program to illustrate the function of infinite loop and give its most unique feature.

09. Describe Arduino functions and using its common syntax to explain all the parts in details.

10. What does it mean to declare a function and give various forms of function declaration?

11. Give the function of array string.

12. What is the meaning of an array bound?

13. Describe the four types of Arduino time functions.

14. Identify a real life application of any of each of the Arduino time functions identified above.

15. What is an array? Explain an industrial setting that could best describe an array.

16. Describe the basic features of an array.

17. Using syntax, explain the process of array declaration

18. Explain how multidimensional arrays are formed and identify where we can use them in real life applications.

Chapter 5

COMMON ARDUINO FUNCTIONS

Chapter Objectives

- By the end of this chapter, the learner should be in a position to:

- Describe fully the I/O functions of Arduino board explaining how to configure the I/O pins.

- Explain what character functions with regards to Arduino programming are and give their significance.

- Highlight various trigonometric functions applied in Arduino IDE

- Expound of the functions from the Math Library which are used in programming of Arduino Boards.

I/O functions

In this section we will understand how the various pins on the Arduino board can be configured to either to accept data (input) or to be used as data output. The pins can be configured to work under different modes as desired by the programmer. Most of the analog pins can easily be configured to so that they accept data. The same method of configuration is applicable for both digital and analog pins as discussed below.

119

Pins Configuration-As INPUT

The function used in pin configuration is **pinMode ( )** though Arduino pins are configured by default to work as inputs. When you configure a pin as an input, it gets to a mode referred to as High-impedance state. Such input pins offer very high resistance equivalent to 100 mega ohms.

The high resistance means very little current to operate an LED connected to this port. Therefore these types of pins are applicable when implementing a capacitive touch sensor or an LED that used as a photodiode.

A pin that has been configured by the function pinMode (pi, INPUT) connected with wires to other circuits or just nothing connected, experiences some noise. The noise is can be as a result of capacitive coupling from a nearby circuit or electrical noise from arising from the environment. This kind of noise causes a random change in the pin state which is very undesirable.

Resistors (Pull-up)

Used when there is no input available, the resistor will steer the pin to a desired state. This is achieved by either adding a pull-up resistor (+5v) or a pull-down resistor (connected to the ground).

When a pin is configured with pull-up resistor, works in a reverse manner like pinMode ( ) function.

Example

```
pinMode(4,INPUT) ; // this function is used to set pin
to input mode minus the use of //built in pull up
resistor
```

```
pinMode(6,INPUT_PULLUP) ; // this function is used to
set pin to input mode through //the use of built in
pull up resistor
```

Pin Configuration-OUTPUT

When a pin is configured by the pinMode ( ) function gets to a state called lo-impedance state. Low impedance provides for an opportunity for such a pin to supply a substantive amount of current to other nearby circuits. Those boards of the ATMEGA type are capable of providing current source (giving out current) and current sink (drawing current) up to an amount of 40 mA. This provides enough power to light an LED and run sensors but insufficient to power relays and motors.

Unfortunately when you try to draw or supply too much current through an output pin, the effect may be devastating even to damage the pin itself. A damaged pin is represented by the term "dead" on the IDE platform. It is only this pin that has been damaged, otherwise all other parts of the Arduino board are functioning properly.

To keep your OUTPUT pin safe, use a 470 ohms or 1000 ohms resistor as part of the output connection. These resistors will restrict the maximum amount of current that can go through the OUTPUT pin. This is in exception of those equipment that require maximum current to run from the Arduino board.

pinMode ( ) function

This is the most commonly used function configuring the Arduino board. The function enables the programmer to configure certain pins so as to be used as either inputs or outputs. To enable the internal pull-up resistors, use the function INPUT_PULLUP though it is automatically disabled by the INPUT mode.

<u>Syntax</u>

```
Void setup ( )

{

pinMode (pin , mode); // gives the name or number of
the pin and the specific mode of operation

}
```

Where : **pin** (specifies the number of pin to be configured

Mode: A pin can be set to INPUT, INPUT_PULLUP or OUTPUT.

<u>Example in a program:</u>

```
int button = 3 ;        // indicates that a button has
been connected to pin

//number 3
int LED = 5;            // indicates that an LED has been
connected to pin

//number 5

void setup ()
{
  pinMode(button , INPUT_PULLUP); // the digital pin is
set as input with

//pull-up resistor

pinMode(button , OUTPUT); // the digital pin is set as
output
```

```
    }
    void setup ()
     {
       If (digitalRead(button )==LOW) // condition for
    pressing button
       {
             digitalWrite(LED,HIGH);  // the code is used
       turn on the LED
             delay(1000);                // delay time is 1000
    ms
             digitalWrite(LED,LOW); // the code is used turn
       off the LED
             delay(1000);                   // delay time is 1000
    ms
         }
    }
```

digitalWrite ( ) function

As the name suggests, this is a function that specifically writes a HIGH or a LOW value to explicitly a digital pin. A pin that was initially configured b the pinMode ( ) function to an OUTPUT state, its voltage will be set to either 5v or 3.3v for HIGH and 0v for LOW state depending on the type of board you are using.

The pinMode ( ) is therefore used before calling the digitalWrite ( ) function otherwise the LED will appear dim. This is because when pinMode ( ) has not been used, the digitalWrite ( ) function automatically activates the internal pull-up resistor which in itself draws large current thereby the LED dims.

Syntax

```
    Void loop()
```

```
{

digitalWrite (pin ,value);

}
```

Explanation: **pin** (specifies the number of pin to be configured

Mode: A pin can be set to INPUT, INPUT_PULLUP or OUTPUT.

Example in a program:

```
int LED = 6;          // indicates that an LED has been
connected to pin

//number 6

void setup ()
{
      pinMode(LED , OUTPUT); // the digital pin is set
as output
}
void setup ()
 {
      digitalWrite(LED,HIGH);   // the code is used
turn on the LED
      delay(1000);            // delay time is 1000
ms
      digitalWrite(LED,LOW); // the code is used turn
off the LED
       delay(1000);             // delay time is 1000
ms
    }
```

AnalogRead ( ) function

When a voltage signal is applied to any of the pins of an Arduino board, it is able to detect this and report through the analogRead ( ) function.

There are six analog pins that enable the board to read the voltages applied to them indicating even the exact amount. AnalogRead ( ) function is supposed to return a value between 0 and 1023 representing voltage levels between 0 and 5 volts. For example, analogRead (0) a value of 512 representing 2.5 volts.

Syntax

```
analogRead(pin);
```

Explanation: **pin** (this value reads between 0 to 5 volts for most boards while on mini and Nano boards, the value reads 0 to 7; on Mega the value reads 0 to 15.

Example on a program

```
int analogPin = 6;//a potentiometer wiper is connected
to analog
//pin number 6 through the middle terminal
int val = 0; // variable called val used to store the
value that has been //read
void setup()

{

    Serial.begin(9600); // setup for serial code

}

Void loop ( )
```

```
{

    Val = analogRead (analogPin);

    Serial.printIn (val); //code for debugging the
    output value
```

Character Functions

Data entry into a computer takes the form of characters which includes letters, special symbols and digits. Therefore in this section we will discuss how C++ programming language manipulates the individual characters.

C++ language has a character-handling library that has several functions used to perform specific tests as a way of manipulating characters. Functions normally receive characters represented as integers which the functions are able to manipulate.

The table below summarizes these functions which are involved in manipulation of character functions represented as a library:

Prototype	Function Explanation
int isdigit(int b)	Function outputs 1 when b is a digit and 0 when it is not.
int isalpha(int b)	Function outputs 1 when b is a letter and 0 when it is not.
int isalnum(int b)	Function outputs 1 when b is a digit or a letter and 0 when it is not.

int isxdigit(int b)	Function outputs 1 when b is a hexadecimal digit character and 0 when it is not.
int islower(int b)	Function outputs 1 when b is a lowercase letter and 0 when it is not.
int isupper(int b)	Function outputs 1 when b is uppercase letter; 0 when it is not.
int isspace(int b)	Function outputs 1 when b is a white-space character—newline ('\n'), space (' '), form feed ('\f'), carriage return ('\r'), horizontal tab ('\t'), or vertical tab ('\v')—and 0 when it is not.
int iscntrl(int b)	Function outputs 1 when b is a control character, such as newline ('\n'), form feed ('\f'), carriage return ('\r'), horizontal tab ('\t'), vertical tab ('\v'), alert ('\a'), or backspace ('\b')—and 0 when it is not.
int ispunct(int b)	Function outputs 1 when b is a printable character apart from a space, a digit, or a letter and 0 when it is not.
int isprint(int b)	Function outputs 1 when b is a printing character apart from space (' ') and 0 when it is not.
int isgraph(int b)	Function outputs 1 when b is a printing character other than space (' ') and 0 when it is not.

Through the examples below, we will be able to learn how to apply these character manipulative functions, that is, isdigit, isalpha, isxdigit and isalnum.

These functions are briefly described below with regards to the type of characters that they manipulate:

Isdigit ( ) function: Concerned with checking whether an argument is a digit ranging from 0 to 9.

Isalpha ( ) function: Checks whether the argument is an uppercase letter (A-Z) or a lowercase letter (a-z).

Isalnum ( ) function: Checks whether the argument is a digit, uppercase letter or a lowercase letter.

Isxdigit ( ) function: Checks whether the argument is a hexadecimal digit that is (A-F, a-f, and 0-9).

Math Library

Arduino has collection of math functions commonly known as math.h used purposely to work on calculations that include floating-point numbers.

These functions are also called Library macros as explained below:

- **M_E**

This function represents the constant e.

The exact value is 2.7182818284590452354.

- **M_LOG2E (/* log_2 e */)**

This function represents the logarithm of the constant e to the base of 2.

The exact value is 1.4426950408889634074

- **M_1_PI (/* 1/pi */**

This function represents the constant 1/pi.

The exact value is 0.31830988618379067154

- **M_2_SQRTPI (/* 2/sqrt(pi) */)**

This function represents the constant /pi.

The exact value is 1.12837916709551257390

- **M_LN10 (/*log_e 10*)**

This function represents the natural logarithm of 10.

The exact value is 2.30258509299404568402

- **M_LN2 (/*log_e 2*)**

This function represents the natural logarithm of 2.

The exact value is 0.69314718055994530942

- **M_LOG10E (/*log_10 e*)**

This function represents the logarithm of e to the base of 10.

The exact value is 0.43429448190325182765

- **M_PI (/*pi*)**

This function represents the constant pi.

The exact value is 3.14159265358979323846

- **M_PI_2 (/*pi/2*)**

This function represents the constant pi/2.

The exact value is 3.3V1.57079632679489661923

- **M_PI_4 (/*pi/4*)**

This function represents the constant pi/4.

The exact value is 0.78539816339744830962

- **M_SQRTI_2 (/* 1/sqrt(2) *)**

This function represents the constant 1/sqrt(2).

The exact value is 0.70710678118654752440

- **M_SQRTI2 (/* sqrt(2) *)**

This function represents the square root of 2.

The exact value is 1.41421356237309504880

- **Acosf:** This macro represents acos ( ) function.

- **Asinf:** This macro represents asin ( ) function.

- **Atan2f:** This macro represents atan2 ( ) function.

- **Cbrtf:** This macro represents cbrt ( ) function

- **Ceilf:** This macro represents ceilf ( ) function

- **Copysignf:** This macro represents copysign( ) function

- **Coshf:** This macro represents cosh ( ) function

- **Expf:** This macro represents exp ( ) function

- **Fabsf:** This macro represents fabs ( ) function

- **Fdimf:** This macro represents fdim ( ) function

- **Floorf:** This macro represents floor ( ) function

- **Fmaxf:** This macro represents fmax ( ) function

- **Fminf:** This macro represents fmin ( ) function

- **Fmodf:** This macro represents fmod ( ) function

- **Frexpf:** This macro represents frexp ( ) function

- **Hypoft:** This macro represents hypot ( ) function

- **INFINITY:** This macro represents the constant infinity.

Other useful mathematics functions are listed below, they also form part of the math.h library:

- **Double acos (double_a):** Function is used to compute the principal value of the arc cosine of _a and return a value between [0, pi] radians. There is an allowable error of [-1, +1].

- **Double asin (double_a):** Function is used to compute the principal value of the arc sine of _a and return a value between [-pi/2, pi/2] radians. There is an allowable error of [-1, +1].

- **Double atan (double_a):** Function is used to compute the principal value of the arc tangent of _a and return a value between [-pi/2, pi/2] radians. There is an allowable error of [-1, +1].

- **Double atan2 (double_a, double_b):** Function is used to compute the principal value of the arc tangent of _a / _b and return a value between [pi/2, pi/2] radians. There is an allowable error of [-1, +1]. The function uses the signs of both arguments to rightly determine the right quadrant for the result.

* **Double cbrt (double_a):** Function is used to compute the principal value of the cube root of _a. There is an allowable error of [-1, +1].

* **Double ceil (double_a):** Function is used identify the smallest integral value that is greater than or equal to _a and return a value that is a floating-point number. There is an allowable error of [-1, +1].

* **Static double copysin (double_a, double_b):** Function is used to return the value of _a with the associated sigh of _b. this function works even in the case of a zero _b.

* **Double cos (double_a):** Function is used to compute the principal value of the arc cosine of _a and return a value between [0, pi] radians. There is an allowable error of [-1, +1].

* **Double cosh (double_a):** Function is used to compute the principal value of the hyperbolic cosine of _a and return a value between [0, pi] radians. There is an allowable error of [-1, +1].

* **Double exp (double_a):** Function is used to compute the exponential value of _a. There is an allowable error of [-1, +1].

* **Double fabs (double_a):** Function is used to compute the absolute value of _a and returns a floating point number.

* **Double floor (double _a):** Function is used identify the largest integral value that is greater than or equal to _a and return a value that is a floating-point number.

* **Double fdim (double __a, double __b):** This function returns the maximum value of (_a- _b, 0). When both _a and _b are null, then the function return NAN.

* **Double fman (double __a, double __b, double_c):** This kind of a function performs a floating-point addition.

* **Double fmax (double __a, double __b):** Function is used identify integral value that is greater between the values _a and _b. When one argument is null, the other is returned and when both are null then the function returns NAN.

* **Double fmin (double __a, double __b):** Function is used identify integral value that is smaller between the values _a and _b. When one argument is null, the other is returned and when both are null then the function returns NAN.

* **Double fmod (double __a, double __b):** Function is calculate the remainder of the value of _a / _b. The function returns a floating-point remainder.

* **Double frexp (double __a, int* __pexp):** Function is meant to break a floating-point number into a fraction which has been normalized and an integer of power 2. The integer is stored in the part pointed by int* _pexp.

* **Double hypot (double __a, double __b):** This returns the length of the hypotenuse of a right triangle. This function is more accurate with least error as compared to the direct formula.

* **Static int isinf (double _a)**: This function returns a non-zero value when _a is finite.

* **Static isinf (double _a)**: This function returns 1 when _a is positive infinity and -1 when _a is a negative infinity.

* **Int isnan (double _a)**: This function returns 1 when _a is a non-object or otherwise zero.

* **Double sqrt (double _a)**: Used to calculate the non-negative square root of _a.

* **Double square (double _a)**: Used to calculate the square of _a.

* **Double tan (double _a):** Used to calculate the tangent of _a in radians.

* **Double tanh (double _a):** Used to calculate the hyperbolic tangent of _a in radians.

* **Double trunc (double _a):** Used to round _a to nearest integer but not to a larger absolute value.

Example in a program:

The example below explain how we can use the math functions above in simple explanations:

```
double double__a = 45.45 ;
double double__b = 30.20 ;
void setup()
{
Serial.begin(9600);
Serial.print("the cos number a = ");
Serial.println (cos (double__a) ); // the code is used
```

```
return the cosine of a
Serial.print("the absolute value of number a = ");
Serial.println (fabs (double__a) ); // calculates the
absolute value of a

//float
Serial.print("the modulus of floating point =");
Serial.println (fmod (double__a, double__b)); //
calculates the modulus of

//the floating-point a
Serial.print("the sine of number a= ");
Serial.println (sin (double__a) ) ;// used to calculate
the sine of a
Serial.print("the square root of number : ");

Serial.println (sqrt (double__a) );// used to calculate
the square root of a

Serial.print("the square root of number a: "); sqrt
(double__a) );// used to //calculate the square root of
a

Serial.println (tan (double__a) ); // used to calculate
the tangent of a

Serial.print("the exponential value of number a : ");
Serial.println ( exp (double__a) ); // function is used
to calculate the the

//exponential value of a.
Serial.print("the cosine of number a: ");


Serial.println (atan (double__a) ); // function used to
calculate arc tangent
```

```
//of a
Serial.print("the tangent of number a: ");
Serial.println (atan2 (double__b, double__a) );// arc
tangent of b/a
Serial.print("the arc tangent of number a: ");
Serial.println (log (double__a) ) ; // code calculates
the natural logarithm

//of a
Serial.print("cos number : ");
Serial.println ( log10 (double__a)); // function meant
to calculate the

//logarithm of a to base 10.
Serial.print("the logarithm of number a to base of 10 :
");
Serial.println (pow (double__a, double__b) );// a is
raised to the power of b
Serial.print("the power of number a : ");
Serial.println (square (double__a)); //calculates the
square of a
}
void loop()
{

}
```

Results

The cosine of number a = 0.10

the absolute value of number = 45.45

the modulus of the floating point =15.25

the sine of number a= 0.99

square root of number: 6.74

tangent of number: 9.67

the exponential value of number: ovf

the cosine number a: 1.55

tangent of number a: 0.59

the arc tangent of number a: 3.82

the cos number a: 1.66

the logarithm of number a to base of 10 : inf

the power of number a: 2065.70

Trigonometric Functions

Trigonometric functions are part of the math library used in practical applications like calculating the distance covered by a moving object or find the angular velocity of a projectile. These functions include: sin, cos, tan, asin, acos and atan as included in Arduino IDE platform. In this section therefore we will look into how to use these functions to solve simple arithmetic problems in real life application.

Syntax

```
double sin (double a); // calculates the sine value of
a in radians
double cos (double b); // calculates the cosine value
of b in radians

double tan (double x); // calculates the tangent value
of x in radians
double acos (double a); //calculates the value of A,
the angle that corresponds to cos (A) = a
double asin (double a); // calculates the value of A,
the angle that corresponds to sin (A) = a

double atan (double a); // calculates the value of A,
the angle that corresponds to tan (A) = a
```

Example in a program

```
double sin = sin(2);   // the approximate value is
0.90929737091
double cos = cos(2); // the approximate value is -
0.41614685058
double tan = tan(2); // the approximate value is -
2.18503975868
```

Chapter Review

- I/O functions:

  * Pins Configuration-As INPUT

  * Resistors (Pull-up)

  * Pin Configuration-OUTPUT

  * pinMode ( ) function

  * digitalWrite ( ) function

  * AnalogRead ( ) function

- Character Functions:

  * Isdigit ( ) function: Concerned with checking whether an argument is a digit ranging from 0 to 9.

  * Isalpha ( ) function: Checks whether the argument is an uppercase letter (A-Z) or a lowercase letter (a-z).

  * Isalnum ( ) function: Checks whether the argument is a digit, uppercase letter or a lowercase letter.

  * Isxdigit ( ) function: Checks whether the argument is a hexadecimal digit that is (A-F, a-f, and 0-9).

- Math Library functions:

  * M_E

  * M_LOG2E (/* log_2 e */)

  * M_1_PI (/* 1/pi */)

  * M_2_SQRTPI (/* 2/sqrt(pi) */)

  * M_LN10 (/*log_e 10*/)

* M_LN2 (/*log_e 2*/)

* M_LOG10E (/*log_10 e*/)

* M_PI (/*pi*/)

* M_PI_2 (/*pi/2*/)

* M_PI_4 (/*pi/4*/)

* M_SQRTI_2 (/* 1/sqrt(2) */)

* M_SQRTI2 (/* sqrt(2) */)

* Double acos (double_a)

* Double asin (double_a

* Double atan (double_a)

* Double atan2 (double_a, double_b)

* Double cbrt (double_a)

* Double ceil (double_a)

* Static double copysin (double_a, double_b)

* Double cos (double_a)

* Double cosh (double_a)

* Double exp (double_a)

* Double fabs (double_a)

* Double floor (double _a)

* Double fdim (double __a, double __b)

* Double fman (double __a, double __b, double_c)

* Double fmax (double __a, double __b)

* Double fmin (double __a, double __b
* Double fmod (double __a, double __b)
* Double frexp (double __a, int* __pexp)
* Double hypot (double __a, double __b)
* Static int isinf (double _a)
* Static isinf (double _a)
* Int isnan (double _a)
* Double sqrt (double _a)
* Double square (double _a)
* Double tan (double _a)
* Double tanh (double _a)
* Double trunc (double _a)
- Trigonometric Functions
  * sin (double a)
  * cos (double b)
  * tan (double x)
  * acos (double a)
  * double asin (double a)
  * double atan (double a)

Assessment

01. What are I/O functions as applied in Arduino programming?

02. Explain the need to configure various pins as either inputs or outputs in an Arduino board,

03. The following I/O functions are used in pin configuration, explain what exactly they do.

a) Pins Configuration-As INPUT

b) Resistors (Pull-up)

c) Pin Configuration-OUTPUT

d) pinMode ( ) function

e) digitalWrite ( ) function

f) AnalogRead ( ) function

4. Using syntax, give the difference between the following I/O functions:

a) digitalWrite ( ) function

b) AnalogRead ( ) function

05. When is a pin said to be "dead". What is the obvious cause of this condition?

06. Using examples, describe the functions of the following functions.

a) Isdigit ( ) function:

b) Isalpha ( ) function:

c) Isalnum ( ) function:

d) Isxdigit ( ) function

07. Give the various trigonometric functions available on Arduino IDE platform.

Chapter 7

INTRODUCTION TO CIRCUIT BUILDING

Chapter Objectives

By the end of this chapter, the learner should be able to:

Explain the general essentials of circuit building in Arduino.

Describe the following processes as applied in Arduino circuit building:

- Prototyping

- Tinkering

- Patching

- Circuit Bending

- Coding

- Planning

- Circuit assembly

Doing it the Arduino Way

Basically Arduino programming involves hands-on duty circuit design where you make your thoughts a reality. It involves making simple and complex designs rather than talk about them. Scientists are ever in the lab trying various means to come up with complex and efficient designs meant to improve life. The search is on for less costly but very powerful prototypes that would be actualized kin the industry and eventually amass great profit. In this chapter, we have explored a variety of options that could help you during your college project especially for the technology students all over the globe.

Perfect engineering work involves strict processes running from A to Z that must be adhered to for a perfect output. Arduino programming presents a journey of discoveries that would blow your mind as you delve much into circuit designs. Programmers must employ passion in this work so as to achieve their goals. The next few pages of this chapter, presents some of the ideologies, philosophies, pioneers work and events that can introduce you into the world of Arduino programming.

Prototyping

This remains the core business of Arduino programming. Designers and programmers over here make circuits and objects that are able to interact with one another, other people and even networks all the world.

Most of the beginners approach this kind of work with a twisted mindset that they have to make all their designs from scratch which is not the case. Such thinking is outdated and should be considered a waste of time. A beginner only need to confirm that some of the circuit components are working properly. Only confirm and move to the next step. This happens thanks to the availability of opportunistic prototypes that have been developed in the labs and readily available on the internet.

Why spend all your resources and time building from scratch, process that will drain your resources and power yet you can pick the same item you are building as ready made in the market. You only need to do what we call "electronics hack", a perfect way to twist the opportunistic prototype to suit your demands. In fact this is a good way to utilize the work well done by big companies and more qualified engineers in the outside world.

Think about James Dyson the father of vacuum cleaners. He had to make a total of 5127 so as to be sure of his product. We cannot do the same in the current civilization.

Planning

Now let talk about what you need to put in place before you begin the real work of circuit design and Arduino programming. Of course, the first thing is to ensure you have the right tools required for the project. First check whether you have an Arduino board that you can easily power through a USB cable or any other power source applicable.

Next thing to check is the Arduino IDE if it is really ready to be used so as to send sketches to the board. Run this program on which ever System Software you are using on your computer. Try checking on the status bar is all the components are well set.

On the hardware side, ensure all the pins are working properly. You can use a simple LED to check whether the pins are alive or dead as was described earlier.

Coding

This involves writing codes in C or C++ programming language on the Arduino IDE platform that would be sent to the board to control its operations. Actually here you will be running two programs, namely, processing sketch and Arduino sketch. The codes for the processing sketch controls most operations of the board. It is readily available over the internet.

For you run the processing sketch successfully, ensure you have done the following: Instruct the operator to generate the font that is being used on the sketch, confirm that the sketch is using the correct serial port when communicating to Arduino board. This you can ascertain by checking on the "tools" menu on the status bar.

Circuit Assembly

This involves putting together all the components that make up your circuit design. Ensure you use 10,000 ohms resistor for most of the circuit resistors though lower values are also applicable apart from the LEDs that require resistors of much lower values. Also remember that LEDs have polarities, that is, they have positive and negative terminals.

Put all your components together clearly noting the power flow in the board to avoid damaging some components that might be wrongly placed. After all the work is done, you will be able to realize a circuit that looks like the on below. Do not forget about your computer where all the coding has been done.

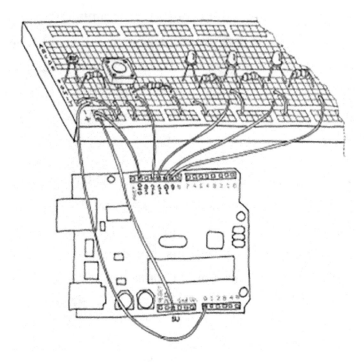

The next procedure is to load all your sketches to the board through the USB connection so that you can begin controlling your circuit. Some of the key points to note in this process of circuit assembly are listed below:

Trim longer wires and those components with very long legs like resistors, diodes and capacitors.

Ensure you have a grounding point which should only be one in case you are using the breadboard.

In case you are having a test lamp, strap the Arduino board than using hot glue stick the Arduino board on the back of the lamp to reduce on the bulkiness of your project.

Finally run your codes and wait to see the response of the lamp. Actually magic takes place until the lamp comes to life.

Tinkering

Actually we all understand the need to play around with technology. Some of these high-tech inventions come out of curiosity. Sometimes it is just okay to explore different possibilities through a variety of projections though without a defined goal. At the end of it all, you may realize something new that could be helpful in future inventions if not in your circuit.

The best way to do this is to utilize the existing technologies as a method of tinkering. A designer should be very curious enough to open the circuits of various toys, try to redesign their circuits and take note of the response. Actually you be learning a lot more than what has been written on the books. Try something like this....!

Circuit Bending

This is another method of tinkering in which low-voltage circuits are short-circuited in order to produce desired effects. This can be done on audio devices such as toys and sound generators. Through this you could be able to learn new tricks of handling electronics. This is quite incredible, it is only through circuit bending that you can create the wildest without necessarily knowing what exactly their purpose is. Enjoy playing around with toys!

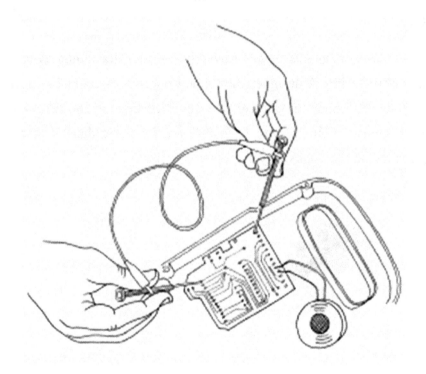

Chapter Review

➤ Doing it the Arduino Way

Basically Arduino programming involves hands-on duty circuit design where you make your thoughts a reality

➤ Prototyping

Designers and programmers over here make circuits and objects that are able to interact with one another, other people and even networks all the world. This happens thanks to the availability of opportunistic prototypes that have been developed in the labs and readily available on the internet.

➤ Planning

Here entails what you need to put in place before you begin the real work of circuit design and Arduino programming.

➤ Coding

This involves writing codes in C or C++ programming language on the Arduino IDE platform that would be sent to the board to control its operations.

➤ Circuit Assembly

This involves putting together all the components that make up your circuit design. Ensure you use 10,000 ohms resistor for most of the circuit resistors though lower values are also applicable apart from the LEDs that require resistors of much lower values

➤ **Tinkering**

Sometimes it is just okay to explore different possibilities through a variety of projections though without a defined goal. At the end of it all, you may realize something new that could be helpful in future inventions if not in your circuit.

➤ **Circuit Bending**

This is another method of tinkering in which low-voltage circuits are short-circuited in order to produce desired effects

Assessment

01. Explain the need to plan before you begin your Arduino work highlighting all the necessary equipment and components that should be put in place.

02. How can a beginner in the world of circuit building benefit from the following practices:

    a. Prototyping

    b. Tinkering

    c. Circuit Bending

03. Explain what coding entails according to Arduino programming.

04. During circuit building, what are the precautions that you need to consider?

05. Name the two basic programming languages mostly used in Arduino IDE platform.

Chapter 8

ARDUINO APPLICATIONS

Chapter Objectives

By the end of this chapter, the learner should be in a position to:

- Explain what entails digital signals both input and output.

- Describe various analog signals both for inputs and outputs

- Explain how Arduino programming can be used in Communications

- Highlight applications of Arduino in regards to sound, timing and mills.

- Describe how to carry out hardware interfacing of Arduino board with other components and microcontrollers.

- Explain how sensors can be used in Arduino circuit building either as actuators or output devices.

Introduction

All the electronics currently in the market use either analog or digital signals in order to perform various procedures and tasks. It is therefore extremely important to understand these two concepts with their finer details before you could begin working on Arduino boards. Also it is equally important to understand the key differences between these signal types especially when handling various components. Think about a motor and sensor both used as output and input devices respectively. The signals used here will be very different and normally opposite of each other.

Digital Input/Output

Digital signals are discrete values that either exists as 1 or 0. This is to mean 1 (High) implies presence of a signal while 0 (Low) represents the absence of a signal. Digital signal is therefore transmitted as binary codes represented by either presence or absence of current, 5v or ground, or presence or absence of a pulse.

Human beings are used to analog signals while robots, computers and most electronic circuits perceive digital signals. As stated earlier, a digital signal only has two states, that is, ON and OFF just like a two-way light switch on your wall.

Digital signals are used everywhere in Arduino programming except for the analog input that is meant specifically to tolerate analog signals. The ON or HIGH state of the digital signal will always equal the board voltage as either 3.3 volts or 5.0 volts. On the other hand, the LOW or OFF state is always represented by 0 volts.

In order to receive or send digital signals on the Arduino board, use only pins labeled 0-13. Again as explained earlier it is possible to set up the analog pins to act as digital pins. This is achievable through the use of the command: pinMode (pin label, value). The pin number here stands for an analog pin ranging from A0-A5, the value in the function is always either input or output.

You can use the same command to set up digital pins. First of all reference the digital pin for pinNumber instead of analog. It is also important to note that digital pins by default used as input pins so it is only required of you to set them to OUTPUT mode. To achieve this, use the command: digitalRead (pin label) where the digital component will be connected to the pin label. digitalRead (pin number) returns either HIGH or LOW as results.

When you want to send a digital signal to a digital pin from the IDE platform, you are supposed to use the code: digitalWrite(pin label, value) where pin label stands for the pin number from which the signal is coming from and the value can either be HIGH or LOW.

Arduino also uses the technique of Pulse Width Modulation to send Digital signal that is in the form of analog. The pin numbers responsible for this are: 3, 5, 6, 9, 10 and 11. And the command used here looks like this: analogWrite(pin label, value). The pin numbers are already provided up there and the value is an integer ranging from 0 (0%) and 100% (255).

Examples of digital signals

ON/OFF, Men's table/Women's table, pregnancy, death, consciousness and the list continues.

Sensors and interfaces used here may include: Relays, Circuit breakers, Switches, Buttons and many others.

Analog Input/Output

Analog signal consists mainly of continuous data inclusive of 0% and 100%. This is what human beings perceive through their senses.

Actually whatever we see and hear are just continuous streams of signals for example the temperature we always feel is never perfectly at a specific point. The values are continuous changing and are never 100% perfectly hot or 100% perfectly cold. Think of a bird singing from a tree nearby, you hear the sound as continuously changing, this stream of data is what constitute analog data. Digital information which in fact is the complementary to analog, represents these streams of data as ones and zeros.

Arduino perceive analog signals as either HIGH (on), LOW (off) or anything relying in between. This implies that for the analog signal, the Arduino voltage can be any value between 0 volts and 5 volts unless otherwise stated or errors. Analog signals are very useful especially when sending and receiving data to and from those instruments that operate on percentages or on mode of ON and OFF. How does this happen in Arduino board?

Arduino with its complexities is able to sample the analog signal sent to its pins and compares these values with the reference value usually 3.3 volts or 5.0 volts. Arduino then signs these voltage levels a special number that lies somewhere between 0 (0%) and 1023 (100%) depending on the exact value of that particular voltage level. Since Arduino system is basically digital, it requires these special numbers so as to use them during various calculations and other tasks involved.

When receiving analog input signals, Arduino board uses pin numbers 0-5 designed specifically to accept analog input from those components that have continuous outputs. For this case, there is no specific set up but when you want read these analog inputs, simply run the code: **analogRead (pin label)** where the pin label represents the pin number unto which the component producing analog output has been connected. As stated earlier, this code should return a number inclusive of 0 to 1023 depending on the voltage level. Also remember what we said about Arduino being able to output digital signal in the form of analog data using Pulse Width Modulation. The output code looks like this: **analogWrite (pin label, value)** where pin label represents the pin number and the value should be an integer ranging between 0 and 225. Arduino UNO have specials pins labelled by a negative sign (-) specifically meant to handle PMW signals.

Examples of analog signals

> Temperature values, level of liquids, speed, time tidal levels, light speed and many more examples.

> Sensors in this case are: Microphone, speedometers, temperature sensors, potentiometers and photoresistors.

Communication

Arduino programming involves certain communication protocols that steer data exchange from the IDE platform and Arduino board. These protocols over here are divided into two categories, that is, parallel and serial. We shall discuss these methods on by one and finally identify where they are best applied.

Parallel Communication

This is a means of communication between Arduino and other peripheral devices using the various input and output ports. The data transfer is only applicable up to a few meters after which the data might be distorted or never reach the destination at all. So for several meters of data transfer, other methods come in since parallel communication becomes obsolete in that case.

In parallel communication, there is transfer of multiple bits simultaneously where the lines of transfer experience crashing waves consisting of 1's and 0's for huge transfer of data.

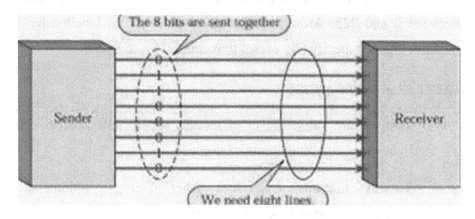

Advantages of parallel Communication

   ❋ Parallel communication is faster than serial communication.

   ❋ Cheap in implementation process.

   ❋ Straightforward and easy to comprehend and utilize.

Disadvantages of parallel Communication

   ❋ Requires many input and output ports together with another of transfer lines.

Serial Communication

Most Arduino boards in the market today are built with different systems involving serial communication.

- Factors that determine the type of communication system include:

- Number of devices that are involved in data transfer with the microcontroller.

- The speed of data transfer.

- The distance separating the devices in the communication network.

- The possibility of simultaneous data transfer, that is, whether it is possible to send and receive data at the same.

Serial Communication modules: **Synchronous-** devices in the network have their own system clocks hence their own timings synchronized with each other.

Asynchronous- Devices in this network have their own clocks but receive triggering pulse from the output of the previous device.

Key terminologies used in data transfer are:

> **Synchronization bits:** These are two or more bits that accompany the packets of data during data transfer process. They start bits and stop bits that are used to mark the beginning and surely the end of a packet of data.

> **Data Bits**: This gives the amount of data in each packet at any specific times between to 9 bits. 8-bit data transfer is the most commonly used size but 7-bit is more preferred for transfer of 7-bit ASCII characters.

Parity Bits: The parity rate should either be odd or even. It is 0 when the number of 1's in the data packet is even and odd when the number of 0's is even.

Baud Rate: Denotes the number of bits that can be transferred through a communication system in a time period of one second.

Examples in programs:

The code written below instructs Arduino to send good morning immediately after it has been started.

```
void setup()
{
Serial.begin(9600);              // serial library baud
rate is set to 9600
Serial.println("good morning"); //codes used to print
good morning
}
void loop()
{

}
```

Once Arduino IDE has started, try opening the serial monitor located at the top right section.

In the top right box provided, type anything and press Enter on your computer. This code sends a number of bytes to the Arduino and the codes below returns after any kind of input:

```
void setup()
{
Serial.begin(9600); // serial library baud rate is set
```

```
up to 9600
}
void loop()
{
if(Serial.available()) //checks whether there are bytes
or characters available for //reading from serial port
    {
        Serial.print("I have not seen anything:"); // used
to print the word 'I have not

//received anything'
        Serial.write(Serial.read()); //section of the
program that sends whatever you

                                        read

    }
}
```

Hardware Interfacing

Arduino uses a special device or feature called Serial peripheral Interface to interconnect with other devices for communication purposes. Serial Peripheral Interface (SPI) consists of four conductors used as follows: conductor one – receiving data, conductor two – sending data, conductor three – synchronization purposes and conductor four – used to selectively select the device that would be connected into the communication network. The four wires used are:

SCK: Connection for the serial clock usually driven by the master board. Connection on pin 13.

MOSI: Connection for the master input which obviously is the slave output and is usually driven by the master. Connection on pin 11

MISO: Connection for the master output which obviously is the slave input and is usually driven by the master. Connection on pin 12

SS: Connection used for selecting the kind of board to be used as slave (Slave Selection). Connection on pin 10.

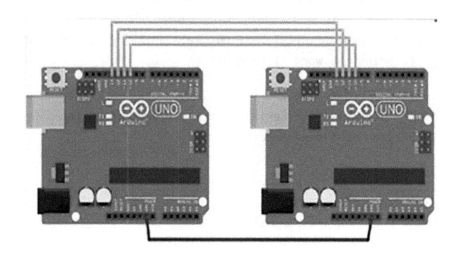

The two examples below illustrate how to set up SPI as master and as Slave Board.

SPI used as the Master board:

```
#include <SPI.h>

void setup (void)

{

   Serial.begin(115200);     // baud rate is to 115200 as
   required by USART

   digitalWrite(SS, HIGH); // this codes is used to
   disable Slave Select

   //conductor
```

```
   SPI.begin ();

   SPI.setClockDivider(SPI_CLOCK_DIV8);//code used to
divide the clock setting //by 8

}

void loop (void)

{

char x;

digitalWrite(SS, LOW); // this code is used to enable
Slave Select conductor


// codes below are used to send test string

for (const char * y = "Hey there!\r" ; x = *y; y++) {

    SPI.transfer (y);

    Serial.print(y);

}

digitalWrite(SS, HIGH); // this code is used to disable
Slave Select conductor

delay(1000);

}



SPI used as the Slave board:

#include <SPI.h>
char buff [78];
```

```
volatile byte indx;
volatile boolean procedure ;
void setup (void)
{

    Serial.begin (115200);

    pinMode(MISO, OUTPUT); //code use to set master as
the output board
    SPCR |= _BV(SPE); //code used to turn on SPI in
slave mode
    indx = 0; //code to set buffer empty
    procedure = false;
    SPI.attachInterrupt(); //code to turn on the
interrupt
}
ISR (SPI_STC_vect) //code indicating SPI interrupt
routine
{ byte b = SPDR; //code used to read a single byte from
SPI Data Register

if (indx < sizeof buff)
  {
    buff [indx++] = b; // instructs board to save data
in the next index as

    an array buff
    if (b == '\r') // confirms if the word has reached
its end
    procedure = true;
  }
}
void loop (void)
{
```

```
if (procedure)
{
    process = false; // the process is instructed to
reset
    Serial.println (buff); // the array is printed as
an output on serial

    monitor
    indx= 0; //the button is reset to zero
}
}
```

NOTE: Arduino interfacing can also take place with other softwares including: Flash, Processing, PD, MaxMSP, VVVV, Director, Ruby and C.

Sensors

♦ Arduino is equally applicable in the field of sensors as shown in the devices below:

♦ Using an Arduino to get readings from potentiometer and from an accelerometer.

♦ Read from an ultra sound sensor

♦ Using two Arduino pins to form a capacitive sensor.

Chapter Review

* Digital Input/Output

  ✓ Digital signals are discrete values that either exists as 1 or 0. This is to mean 1 (High) implies presence of a signal while 0 (Low) represents the absence of a signal.

* Analog Input/Output

  ✓ Analog signal consists mainly of continuous data inclusive of 0% and 100%. This is what human beings perceive through their senses. Actually whatever we see and hear are just continuous streams of signals for example the temperature we always feel is never perfectly at a specific point

* Communication

  ✓ Parallel Communication

  ✓ Serial Communication

* Asynchronous- Devices in this network have their own clocks but receive triggering pulse from the output of the previous device.

* Synchronization bits: These are two or more bits that accompany the packets of data during data transfer process. They start bits and stop bits that are used to mark the beginning and surely the end of a packet of data.

* Key terminologies used in data transfer are:

  ✓ Data Bits

166

✓ Parity Bits

✓ Baud Rate

✱ Hardware Interfacing

✓ Arduino uses a special device or feature called Serial peripheral Interface to interconnect with other devices for communication purposes. Serial Peripheral Interface (SPI)

Assessment

1. Explain the meaning of digital and analog signals as applied in Arduino programming.

2. Give three examples of electronic devices that produce or accept digital and analog data signals respectively.

3. What is the significance of Pulse Width Modulation pins in an Arduino board?

4. Name the two methods of communication that are applied in Arduino programming explaining their various merits and demerits.

5. Distinguish between synchronous and asynchronous methods of communication.

6. Describe the meaning of the following terms:

a. Data Bits

b. Parity Bits

c. Baud Rate

7. Explain what SPI entails and give its significance in hardware interfacing in Arduino programming.

Chapter 9

BASIC DIGITAL ARDUINO PROGRAMS

Chapter Objectives

At the end of this chapter, the learner should be able to:

- Write and run codes to initiate the following simple projects:

  - ➤ LED Blink

  - ➤ LED Blink without Delay

  - ➤ LED Blink with Delay

  - ➤ Arduino Button

  - ➤ Arduino Pushbutton (Debounce)

  - ➤ Creating a Loop

LED Blink

This is the most basic program in Arduino programming just like printing the word "hello world" in any other programming language. Since in Arduino programming there is no screen to print "hello world", we therefore blink an LED as our first test program. This is indeed a very simple program that is meant to give you a strong foundation as you invest into the world of circuit building through prototyping.

The Required Components

- o One breadboard

- o An Arduino Uno

- o One LED

- o Resistor (330 ohms)

- o Two jumper wires

Circuit

The circuit is quite simple due to the small number of components, therefore just follow the simple circuit diagram below:

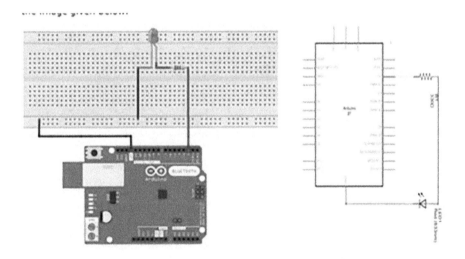

Finding the polarity of the LED

An LED has polarity, that is, negative and positive terminals. To determine this, hold the LED with the flat side facing you. The shorter leg on your left side is the negative terminal while the longer leg on your right is the positive terminal.

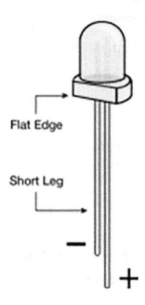

Flat Edge

Short Leg

−

+

Sketch

Quickly open the Arduino IDE on your computer, then a new sketch file on the New tab then begin writing your codes as shown below:

*/ Blink an LED, the codes below are meant to turn a Light Emitting Diode connected to a digital pin periodically. Pin number 13 is used since it has a resistor in its circuit to limit current through the LED */

```
int ledPin = 13; // LED has been connected to digital
pin number 13
void setup()
{
   ledPin(pinMode, OUTPUT); // the digital pin is set as
the output
 }
void loop()
 {
   digitalWrite(pinMode, HIGH); // the code is used to
```

```
set LED ON
  delay(1000); // delay time is a second
  digitalWrite(ledPin, LOW); // the code is used to set
LED OFF
  delay(1000); // delay time is a second
}
```

LED Blink without Delay

Sometimes you may wish to let the LED light without stopping and this calls for the use of another function other than delay ( ). The function for LED blinking without delay keep track of the time when the LED was turned ON and OFF. The using a loop ( ), it checks if sufficient time interval has passed so as to turn the LED ON if it was OFF and vice versa. The other components are the same as for the example above.

Here are the codes:

```
int ledPin = 13; // an LED has been  connected to a
digital pin number 13

int num = LOW; // int num has been declared and
assigned LOW representing LED //previous value

long previousMillis = 0; // stores the value for when
the LED was last updated

long delay = 1000; // delay time is set to one second
(milliseconds)

void setup()

{
```

```
    pinMode(ledPin, OUTPUT); // the digital pin is set
to be the OUTPUT

}

void loop()

{

// the codes are the ones to control the lighting of
the LED.

if (millis() - previousMillis > delay)

    {

    previousMillis = millis(); // recalls the previous
time the LED blinked

// the codes below turns the LED ON in case it was OFF
and vice-versa.

if (num == LOW)

    num = HIGH;

else

    num = LOW;

    digitalWrite(ledPin, num);

    }

}
```

Fading an LED

For this case we will be using the analogWrite ( ) function to initiate the fading process an LED connected to the Arduino board. This is possible because analogWrite ( ) function uses Pulse Width Modulation technique which is able to turn on and off a digital pin quickly in different ratios thereby creating the fading effect. The components are still the same with the first example including the circuit. The only difference is noticed in the codes as shown below:

/*

Fade

This example illustrates the use of the function analogWrite ( ) to control the fading of an LED*/

```
int ledPin = 6;      // LED is attached to the PMW pin
number 6

int brightness = 0; // current brightness of the LED

int fadeStep = 6; // the number of steps to fade the
LED through


void loop()
  {
      //code used to set the brightness of the LED on
pin 6:
   analogWrite(ledPin, brightness);
      //code meant to change LED brightness for the next
step through the
      //loop:
```

173

```
brightness = brightness + fadeStep;

   //codes used to reverse the fading direction at the
ends of each previous

 //fade:

 if (brightness == 0 || brightness == 255)

   {

       fadeStep = -fadeStep ;

   }

   // our delat time is 30 milliseconds so as to realize
the dimming effect

 delay(300);

}
```

Arduino Button

This is typically a button that connects two points in a circuit. When pressed, the button completes the circuit between these two points as in lighting an LED.

Components

  + A pushbutton

  + One Arduino Uno

  + One Light Emitting Diode

  + Three connecting wires.

  + 2.2 kilo ohms

Procedure

Your circuit should look like the one below:

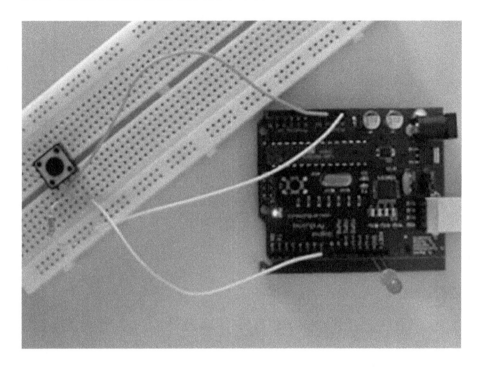

The codes for this project are written below:

```
int outPin = 14; // the LED has been connected to pin
number 14

int inPin = 3; // our input pin for a pushbutton will
be pin number 3

int num = 0; // variable declaration; used to read the
pin status

void setup() {

    pinMode(outPin, OUTPUT); // LED will be used as the
OUTPUT
```

```
    pinMode(inPin, INPUT); // pushbutton shall be our
INPUT for this case

}

void loop()

  {

     num = digitalRead(inPin); // the code is used to
read value of the input

    if (num == HIGH) { // checks whether the button is
released (HIGH input)

    digitalWrite(outPin, LOW); // turns OFF the LED

  }

else

  {

  digitalWrite(outPin, HIGH); // turns the LED ON

  }

}
```

Arduino Pushbutton as a Debounce

This example is similar to the above exercise apart from the function of the pushbutton. The pushbutton debounces the input that is to mean without pressing the button represents a code similar to multiple presses.

The components and the circuit board is the same as the above example. So we will go direct to the codes as that we highlight the difference.

Code

```
int inPin = 6;        // the input has been assigned to
pin number 6

int outPin = 11;      // the output has been assigned to
pin number 11


int position = HIGH; // shows the current state of the
output pin number 11

int display; //indicates the current reading of the
input pin number 6

int previous = LOW; // the previous reading the input
pin assigned LOW


long time = 0; // the variable time represents the
period when the output was //toggled

long debounce =100; // the debounce time has been
assigned

void setup()

{

    pinMode(inPin, INPUT);

    pinMode(outPin, OUTPUT);

}

void loop()

 {

   display = digitalRead(inPin);
```

```
if (display == HIGH && previous == LOW && millis() -
time > debounce) {

  // ... the function returns an inverted output

if (position == HIGH)

    position = LOW;

  else

    position = HIGH;

// ... function recalls the time when button was
pressed

time = millis();

  }

digitalWrite(outPin, position);

previous = display;

}
```

Creating a Loop

Components required

- Six Light Emitting Diodes

- Six 220 Ohm resistors

- Seven jumper wires

- One Arduino Uno

In this example we shall six LEDs to demonstrate sequential blinking using the function digitalWrite(pin label, LOW/HIGH) together with delay ( ).

178

Circuit

Code

```
int timer = 120; // timing reduces with an increase in
the time number.

int pins[] = { 2,3, 4, 5, 6, 7, 8 }; // pin numbers as
an array of

int value_pins = 6; // array length represented by the
number of pins

void setup()

{

   int j;

for (j = 0; j< value pins; j++) // the array elements
as numbered from 0 //to value_pins - 1

pinMode(pins[j], OUTPUT); // each pin has been set as
an output

}

void loop()

{
```

```
int j;

for (j = 0; j < num_pins; j++)

    {

// a loop is set through each output pin...

digitalWrite(pins[j], HIGH); // function to turn the
output pin    ON,

delay(timer);                    // delay function,

digitalWrite(pins[j], LOW); // function to turn the
output pin OFF

        }

for (j = value_pins - 1; j >= 0; j--)

    {

digitalWrite(pins[j], HIGH);

delay(timer);

digitalWrite(pins[j], LOW);

        }

}
```

Chapter Review

LED Blink: The Required Components

- One breadboard

- An Arduino Uno

- One LED

- Resistor (330 ohms)

- Two jumper wires

Finding the polarity of the LED

> An LED has polarity, that is, negative and positive terminals. To determine this, hold the LED with the flat side facing you. The shorter leg on your left side is the negative terminal while the longer leg on your right is the positive terminal.

Fading an LED

> This is possible because analogWrite ( ) function uses Pulse Width Modulation technique which is able to turn on and off a digital pin quickly in different ratios thereby creating the fading effect.

Arduino Button

> This is typically a button that connects two points in a circuit. When pressed, the button completes the circuit between these two points as in lighting an LED.

Arduino Pushbutton as a Debounce

> This example is similar to the above exercise apart from the function of the pushbutton. The pushbutton debounces the input that is to mean without pressing the button represents a code similar to multiple presses.

Creating a Loop

> This project involves using six LEDs to demonstrate sequential blinking using the function digitalWrite (pin label, LOW/HIGH) together with delay ( ).

Assessment

1. What is the function of the resistor used in LED blinking project?

2. Differentiate using functions between fading and LED and LED blink project.

3. Write a simple program to illustrate the use of a pushbutton in Arduino project.

4. Draw a simple diagram of an LED and show the polarity of its terminals.

5. What is the function of an Arduino button?

6. Using real life examples highlight the difference between a normal Arduino button and a pushbutton.

7. Write and explain the parts of a function used to create a sequential blinking of LEDs in an Arduino project.

Chapter 10

BASIC ANALOG ARDUINO PROGRAMS

Chapter Objectives

By the end of this chapter, the learner should be in a position to:

➢ Implement the following simple projects using Arduino kit

❖ Analog input

❖ Knock sensor

❖ Arduino smoothing

❖ Printing an analog input through a method of graphing

Analog Input

In this project we shall use a potentiometer as the source of analog input signal to the Arduino board. Ideally, the potentiometer is able to vary resistance (variable resistance) which can then be read by the Arduino board as analog input. We are going to use the already fixed LED pin 11 on the Arduino board as part of our project.

Components required

✳ A potentiometer

✳ An Arduino project for LED lighting

✳ Three jumper wires

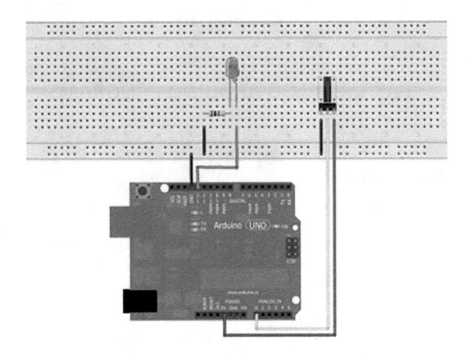

Sketch

/* potentiometer project under AnalogInput

This project aims to turn ON and OFF a light Emitting Diode periodically. The amount of light of the LED depends on the value of resistance of the potentiometer used. Increasing resistance reduces the amount of light and vice versa.

*/

```
int num  = 0; //this variable stores the input value
from the sensor output, //initially assigned 0

void setup()

{
```

```
pinMode(ledPin, OUTPUT); // function declares the LED
as an OUTPUT

}

void loop()

{

num = analogRead(inPin);      // function to read the
value of sensor //output

digitalWrite(ledPin, HIGH);   // function to turn the
LED ON

delay(num);                   // delay function to stop the
program for a while

digitalWrite(ledPin, LOW);    // function to turn OFF
the LED

delay(num);                            // function stops the
program for a while

}
```

Knock Sensor

For this kind of a project, we shall employ the use of a piezo element and trap its sound as the analog input into the Arduino board. The processor of the board is able to read analog signals with the aid of its ADC (analog to digital Converter). The Piezo element (knock sensor) is just but an electronic device that is capable of playing tones and detect tones at the same. The Arduino board detects the sound levels as voltage levels, transform the voltage level to a corresponding value ranging from 0 to 1024 for voltages of 0 to 5.0 volts.

Remember that the Piezo element has polarity, black wire representing the negative terminal while the red wire represents the positive terminal.

In the sketch, we will try to capture the sound level (knock) of the Piezo element and confirm that it is above a certain threshold then send a "Knock" string a signal to the Arduino IDE platform.

<u>Circuit</u>

<u>Sketch</u>

/* Knock Sensor

In this project we are using the Piezo element as a knock sensor. We therefore have to listen to the sound level, if the signal goes beyond a specified threshold. The sketch sends "knock" string to the serial port when the threshold is crossed, and then toggles the LED connected on pin number 12.

```
*/

int ledPin = 13; // led connected to control pin 13

int knockSensor = 0; // the knock sensor to be
connected at analog pin number //0

byte num = 0; // variable num shall be used to store
the input value from the //sensor pin

int statePin = LOW; // variables statePin used to store
the last LED status //and also to toggle the light

int THRESHOLD = 120; // threshold value that will
determine whether the detected //sound is a knock or
not

void setup()

{

  pinMode(ledPin, OUTPUT); // function declares the
ledPin as the OUTPUT

  Serial.begin(9600); // indicate the use of serial
port

}

void loop()

{

  num = analogRead(knockSensor); // function is used to
read the value of the  //sensor and store it in the
variable num
```

```
if (num >= THRESHOLD)

    {

statePin = !statePin; // function that is used to
toggle the status of the ledPin though it does not use
time cycle

digitalWrite(ledPin, statePin); // function to turn LED
ON or OFF

Serial.println("Knock!"); // function sends the string
"Knock!" through //the serial port to the computer then
a newline

delay(100); // a very short delay in order to prevent
serial port from //overloading

    }

}
```

Arduino Smoothing

Involves the use of arrays where the sketch is supposed to read analog input repeatedly, calculate the running average and finally print the result.

<u>Sketch</u>

```
int readings[VALUES];        // array declaration to
represent readings from the //analog input

int index = 0;        // variable declaration and
initialization

int total = 0;        // variable declaration and
initialization
```

```
int    average    =    0;    //    variable    declaration    and
initialization

int    inputPin    =    0;    //    variable    declaration    and
initialization

void setup()

{

 Serial.begin(9600);  //  function  used  to  create  a
serial communication with the //computer

for (int j = 0; j < VALUES; j++)

readings[j] = 0; //setting  all the initial readings to
0

}

void loop()

{

   total -= readings[index]; // code to subtract the
last reading

   readings[index]  =  analogRead(inputPin);  //  read
input value from the sensor

   total += readings[index]; code that adds the reading
to the total

   index = (index + 1); // index increment by one

if (index >= VALUES) // initiate only at the end of the
array...

   index = 0;           // ...return back to the array
beginning
```

```
    average = total / VALUES; // code to get the average
value

    Serial.println(average); // prints the OUTPUT ASCII
on the computer IDE              //platform

}
```

Printing Analog Input (Graphing)

This project demonstrate the how to read analog data, convert the signal into voltage levels and finally print t.

Components Required

- One breadboard

- One Arduino Uno

- One Potentiometer 5 kilo ohms

- Two jumper wires

- Eight LEDs

Circuit

The circuit diagram and the components on the diagram are shown below:

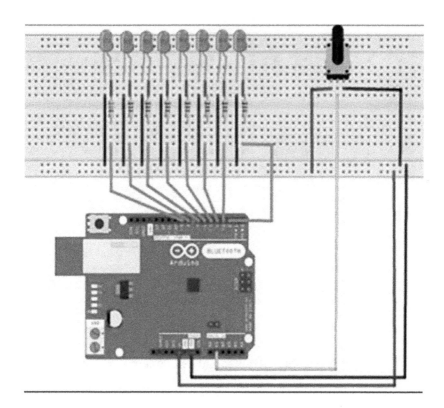

Sketch

```
*/

// the constants used below are to remain the same all
through:

const int analogPin = A0; // the potentiometer has been
attached to this pin

const int ledCount = 8;   // representing the number of
pins that will produce //the graphing effect

int ledPins[] = {3, 4, 5, 6, 7, 8, 9, 10}; // pin
numbers where the LEDs will //be attached forming an
array of pins

void setup()
```

```
{

    // a loop over the pin array thereby setting them as
the OUPUT:

for (int firstLed = 0; firstLed < ledCount; firstLed++)

    {

        pinMode(ledPins[firstLed], OUTPUT);

    }

}

void loop()

{

    // the code below reads the potentiometer output to
use as the system input:

int sensorOutput = analogRead(analogPin);

// copy the result to a range of LEDs from 0 to 7:

int ledLevel = map(sensoroutput, 0, 1023, 0, ledCount);

// a loop over the pin array:

for (int firstLed = 0; firstLed < ledCount; firstLed++)

{

// when the array element has an index which is less
than ledLevel then

// turn ON the pin for this particular element:

if (firstLed < ledLevel)
```

```
        {

    digitalWrite(ledPins[firstLed], HIGH);

        }

// function to turn OFF all other pins whose array
element have indices higher      //than the ledLevel:

    else

        {

        digitalWrite(ledPins[firstLed], LOW);

        }

    }

}
```

It is equally important to NOTE the results of this project: The eight LEDs will turn ON one after another with an increase in the value of the analog reading and they will be again turning OFF one by one on decreasing the value of analog reading.

Chapter Review

In this chapter we have been able to learn a variety of projects where analog signals are used as the system input as summarized below:

➤ Analog Input

 ❖ In this project we 1 use a potentiometer as the source of analog input signal to the Arduino board. Ideally, the potentiometer is able to vary resistance (variable resistance) which can then be read by the Arduino board as analog input. We are going to use the already fixed LED pin 11 on the Arduino board as part of our project.

Components required

 ❖ A potentiometer

 ❖ An Arduino project for LED lighting

 ❖ Three jumper wires

➤ Knock Sensor

 ❖ For this kind of a project, we employ the use of a piezo element and trap its sound as the analog input into the Arduino board. The processor of the board is able to read analog signals with the aid of its ADC (analog to digital Converter). The Piezo element (knock sensor) is just but an electronic device that is capable of playing tones and detect tones at the same.

➢ Arduino smoothing

❖ Involves the use of arrays where the sketch is supposed to read analog input repeatedly, calculate the running average and finally print the result.

➢ Printing Analog Input (Graphing)

❖ This project demonstrate the how to read analog data, convert the signal into voltage levels and finally print t.

Components Required

❖ One breadboard

❖ One Arduino Uno

❖ One Potentiometer 5 kilo ohms

❖ Two jumper wires

❖ Eight LEDs

Assessment

1. Explain how a potentiometer can be used as an analog input and how an Arduino board manipulates this signals and sends a print out to the IED platform.

2. Using a simple describe the use of a potentiometer to control the intensity of light in an Arduino controlled circuit.

3. What is Arduino smoothing?

4. You have been provided with the following components:

- o One breadboard

- o One Arduino Uno

- o One Potentiometer 5 kilo ohms

- o Two jumper wires

- o Eight LEDs

Describe how you will connect them to realize a graphing effect in Arduino programming.

Chapter 11

TROUBLESHOOTING

Chapter Objectives

In this final chapter, the learners are expected to be able to:

01. Describe the process of Arduino board testing

02. Explain the details of circuit testing in a breadboard

03. Identify various problems that are associated with Arduino circuits

04. Explain how to isolate and solve the challenges with Arduino circuits

05. Successfully seek online help in case of redundant problems.

Arduino Board Testing

In the process of circuit building, there will come a time when nothing will be working. This moment will call for a process of troubleshooting and debugging in order to identify and solve the problems with your experiment.

Key points to a successful troubleshooting:

Understanding: Always ensure that you properly understand all the components used in your experiment. Clearly mark out the power flow all these components are connected with one another.

Simplification and Segmentation: This is more like divide and rule tactic where you break down the project and figure out the problem with each and every component

Exclusion and Certainty: This involves investing each part separately and being sure of their functionality. Through this you will be able ascertain the problem with each component.

Board testing therefore involves "Blinking an LED", if it does not work, check on the USB connection and other more options explored below.

Breadboard Circuit Testing

Run a short circuit test by connecting your Arduino board to the breadboard. If the PWR LED turns OFF then there is a serious short circuit connection on your board. Quickly begin segmentation and simplification to find the wrong connection.

Problem Identification

Some of the common problems with Arduino programming are listed below:

* Arduino IDE not launching: Use the *run.bat* files as alternative option.

* Windows Operating System assigning a COM port which is greater to Arduino: Solve this by convincing windows to assign

a lower COM port. For other versions of Windows, follow the procedures described earlier in this book about *Port Identification*.

Problem Isolation and Solving

This option provides for you to reproduce a problem. When your circuit exhibits some problems, find out the exact place and place (component) associated with that particular problem. This will help you to correctly describe a problem and possibly suggest a solution.

Online Help

In case the above suggestions do no work, you are welcomed to seek online help on the Arduino website: www. Arduino.cc/en/Guide. While seeking online help, be sure to specify the following parameters:

- The type of Arduino board you are using.

- The Operating System you are using to run Arduino IDE.

- Give a general description of your problem.

- Of course use CAPITALS to specify all these.

Chapter Review

- ➤ Arduino Board Testing

Key points to a successful troubleshooting:

- ✓ Understanding:

- ✓ Simplification and Segmentation

- ✓ Exclusion and Certainty

- ➤ Breadboard Circuit Testing

  - ✓ Run a short circuit test by connecting your Arduino board to the breadboard

- ➤ Problem Identification

  - ✓ Arduino IDE not launching.

  - ✓ Windows Operating System assigning a COM port which is greater to Arduino.

- ➤ Problem Isolation and Solving

  - ✓ This option provides for you to reproduce a problem.

- ➤ Online Help

  - ✓ Arduino website: www. Arduino.cc/en/Guide.

Assessment

1. Explain the use of *run.bat* files in Arduino launching.

2. What is the major aim of carrying out segmentation and certainty in circuit troubleshooting?

3. Give the advantage of problem isolation in identifying challenges with Arduino circuits.

www.ingramcontent.com/pod-product-compliance
Lightning Source LLC
Chambersburg PA
CBHW071116050326
40690CB00008B/1238